Dead Things

A Picture Book

By: Ashley J. Horton

WARNING

READER DISCRETION IS ADVISED

This book is not for the faint of heart, and contains images some might find disturbing.

A note from the author:

Please note that all of these animals were already dead and were not harmed by me.
This book began both as a coping mechanism and as a joke.
I started taking pictures of dead animals I found at work because it made me sad. Art in some form has been my healthiest coping skill. I find lots of dead birds due to glass windows where I work, the other animals I find at work are often displaced due to construction. I have also sought out roadkill and dabbled in taxidermy.

The reason I say this book started as a joke is because one day I posted on social media, "I should publish a book called Dead Things A Picture Book". Many of my weird friends said, "I'd buy that!"

So here we are.

I would also like to thank my supportive wife, friends, and family, who have made phone calls and sent texts telling me where dead things are, driven with me to look for road kill, gone with me to a taxidermy class, have brought me bones and other bits, and helped edit this book. I thank you, and also recognize you may not want to be named.

-Ash

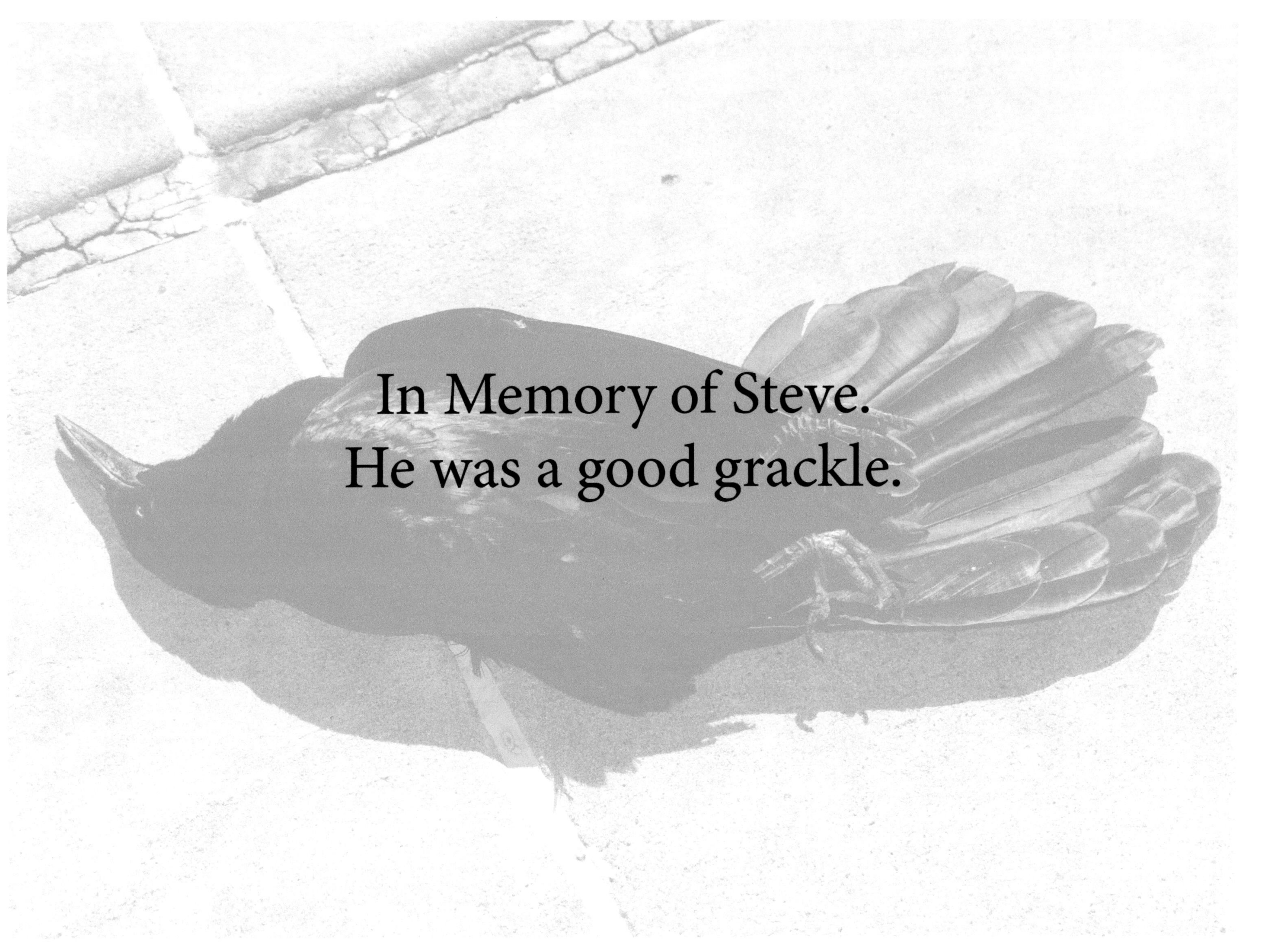

In Memory of Steve.
He was a good grackle.

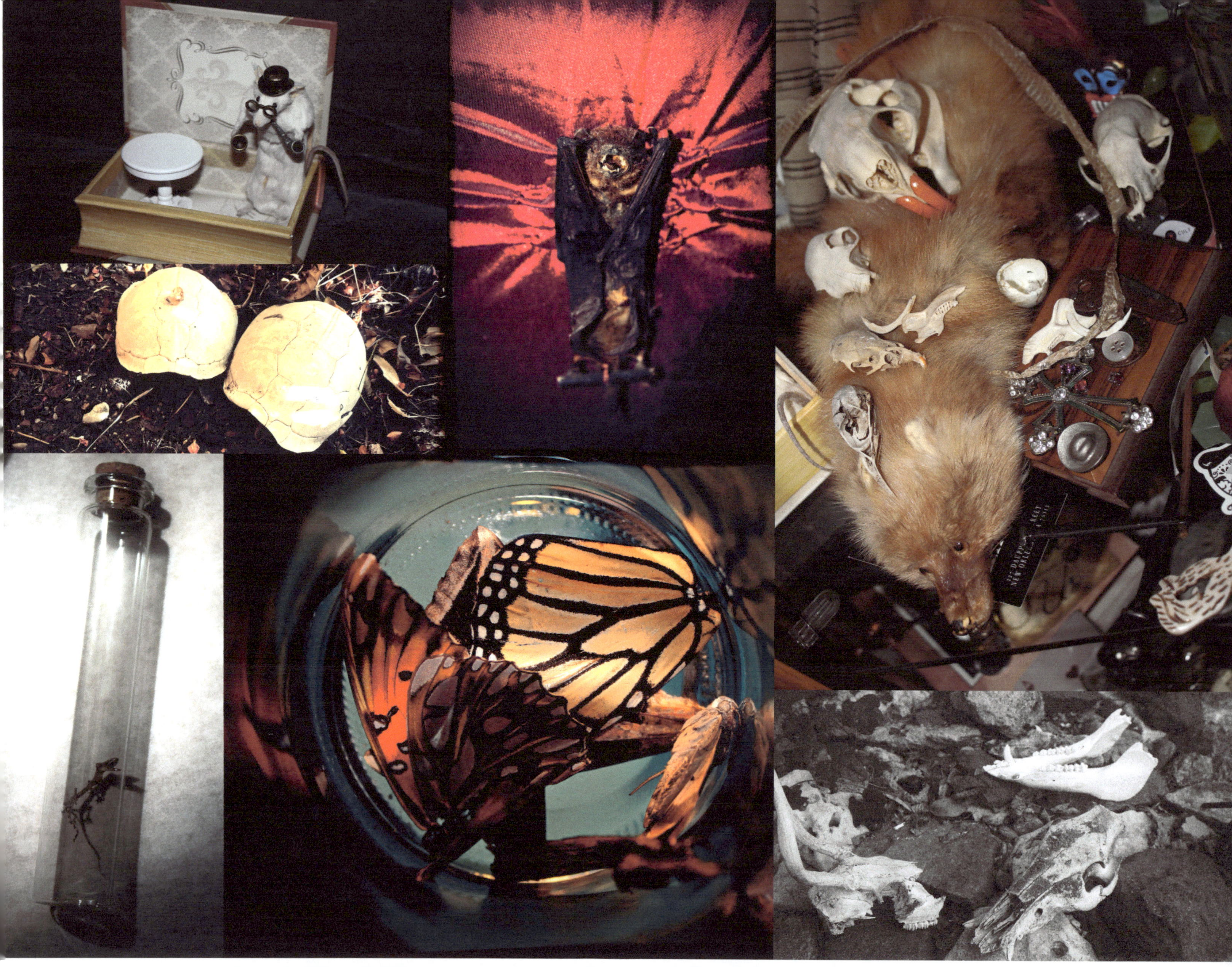

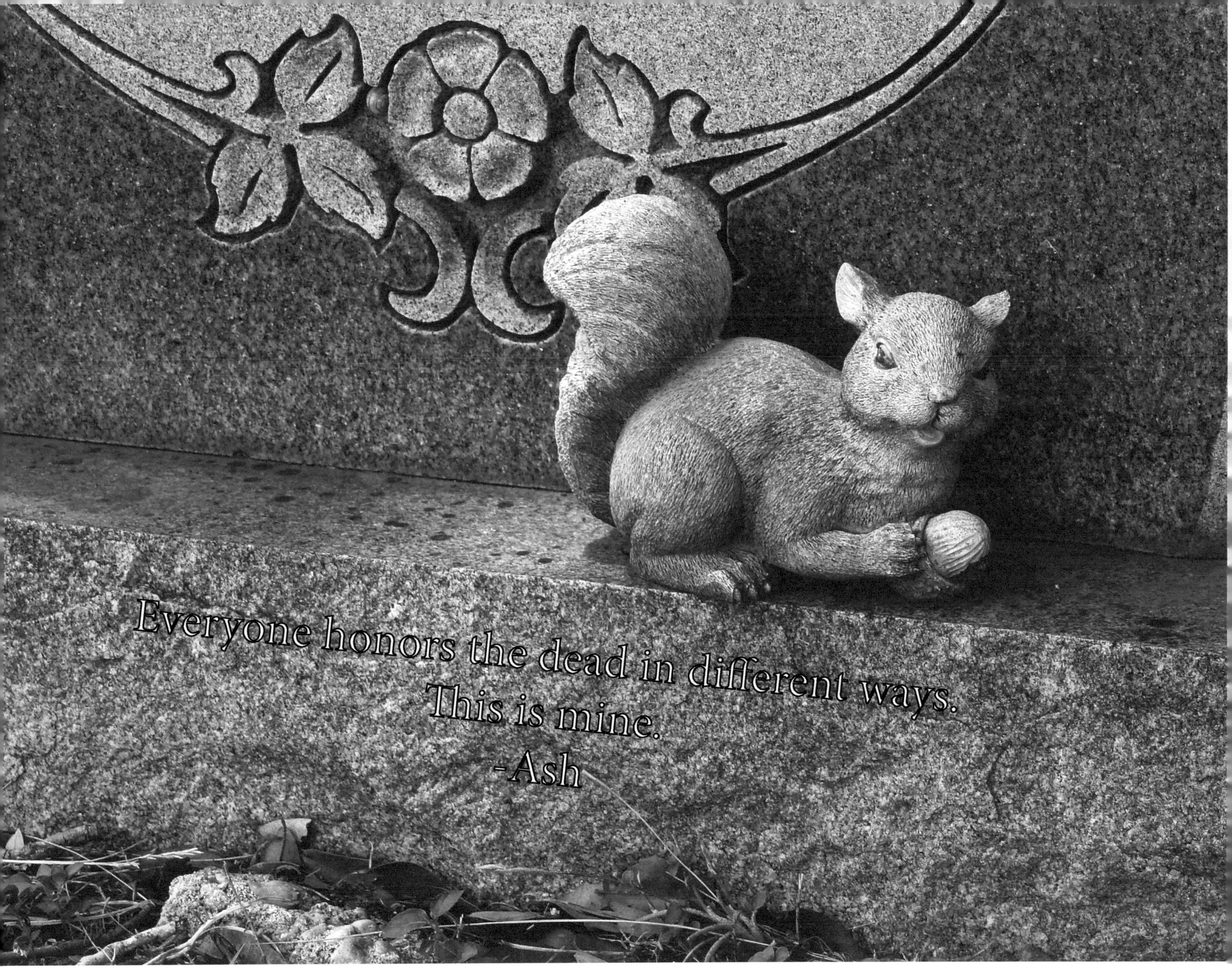

Everyone honors the dead in different ways.
This is mine.
-Ash

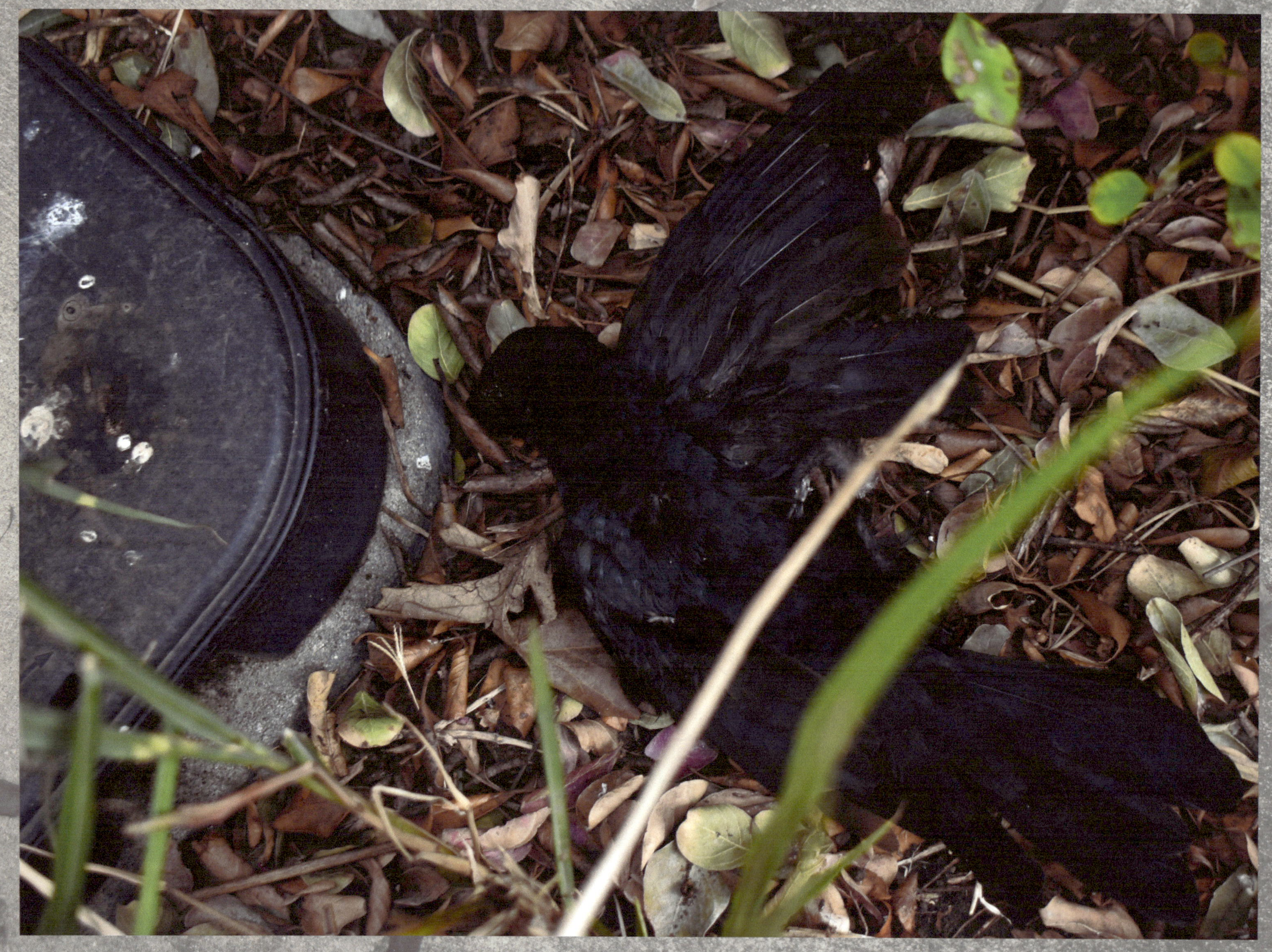

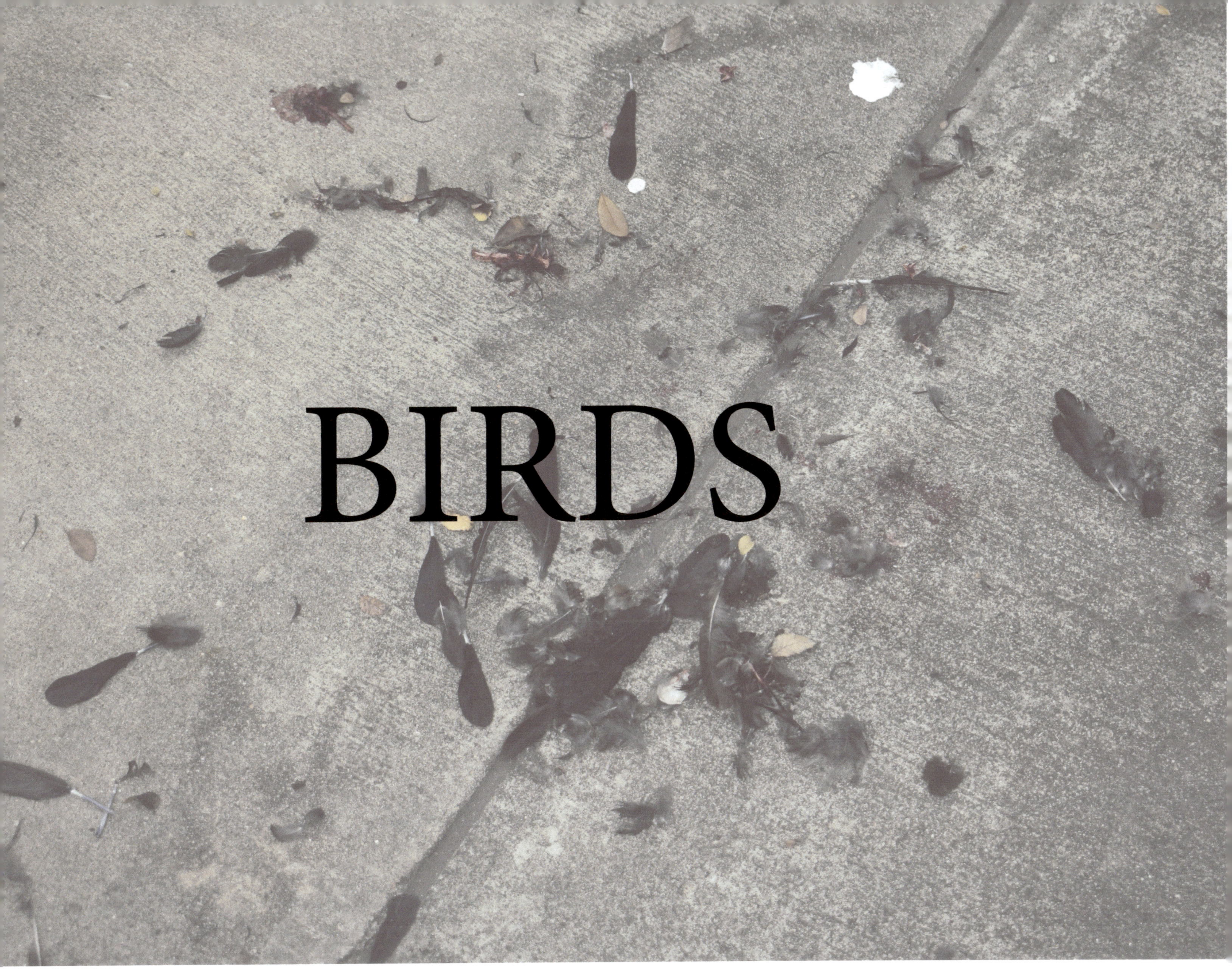
BIRDS

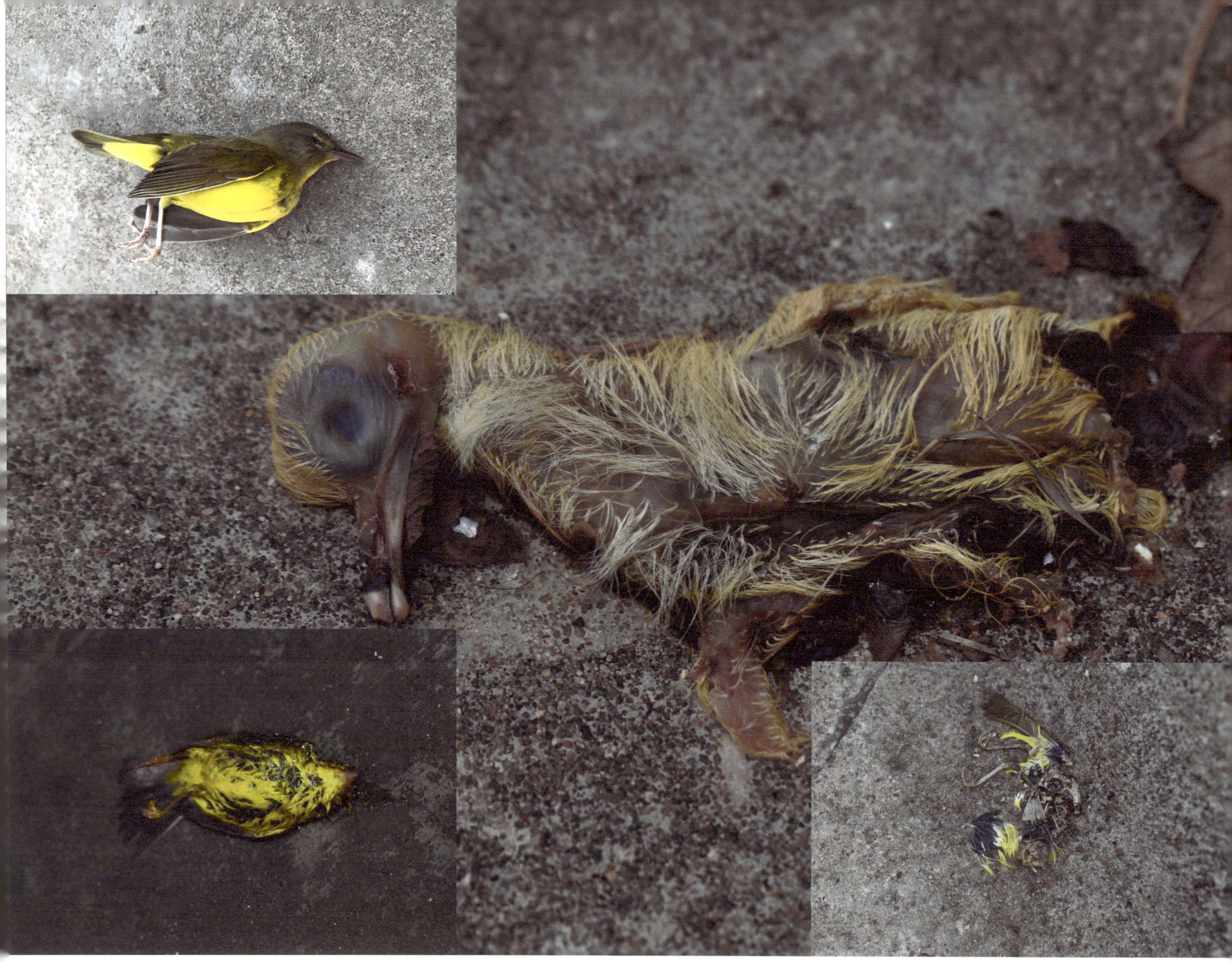

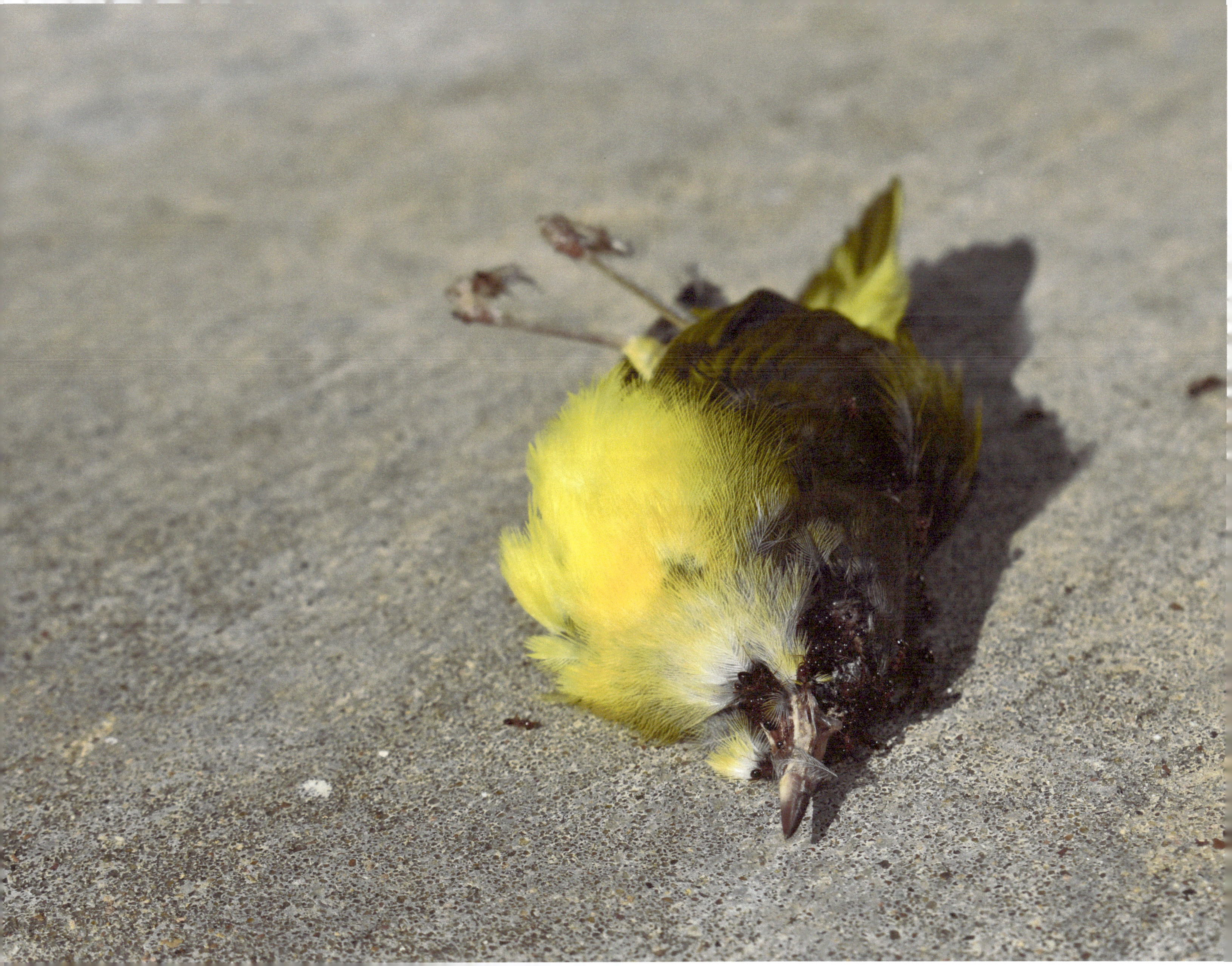

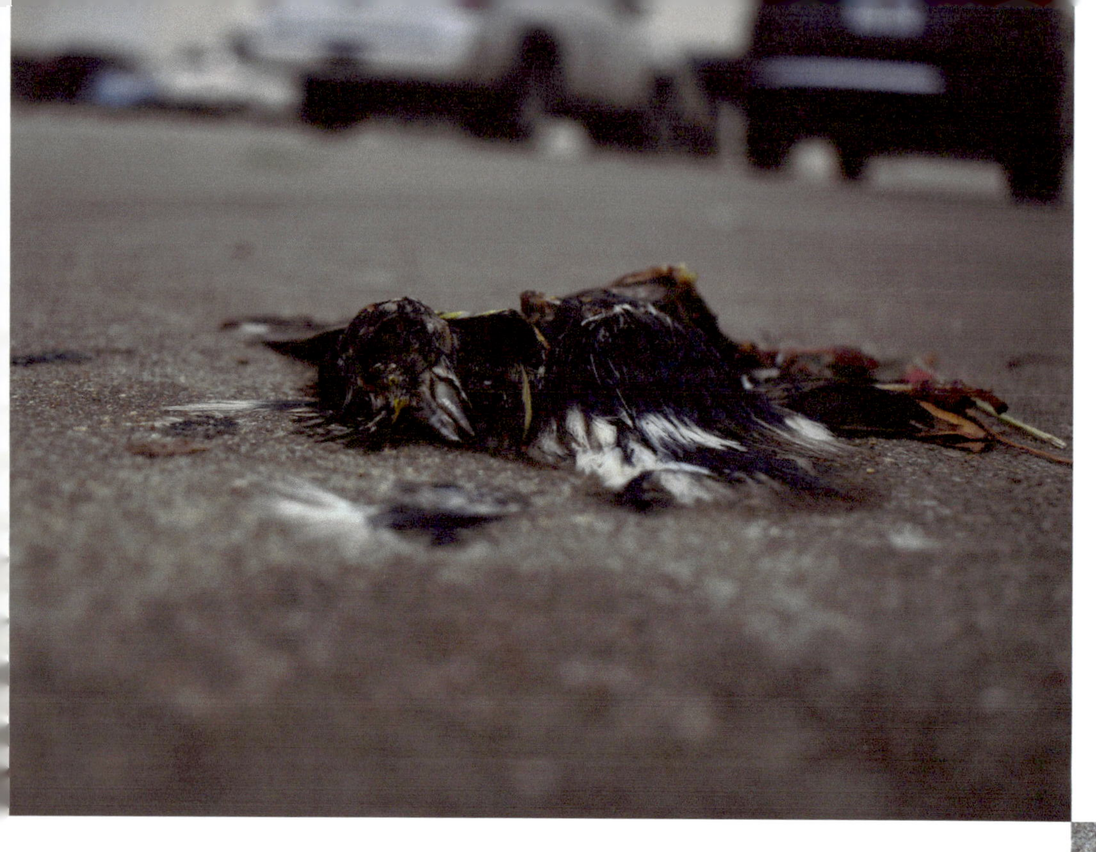

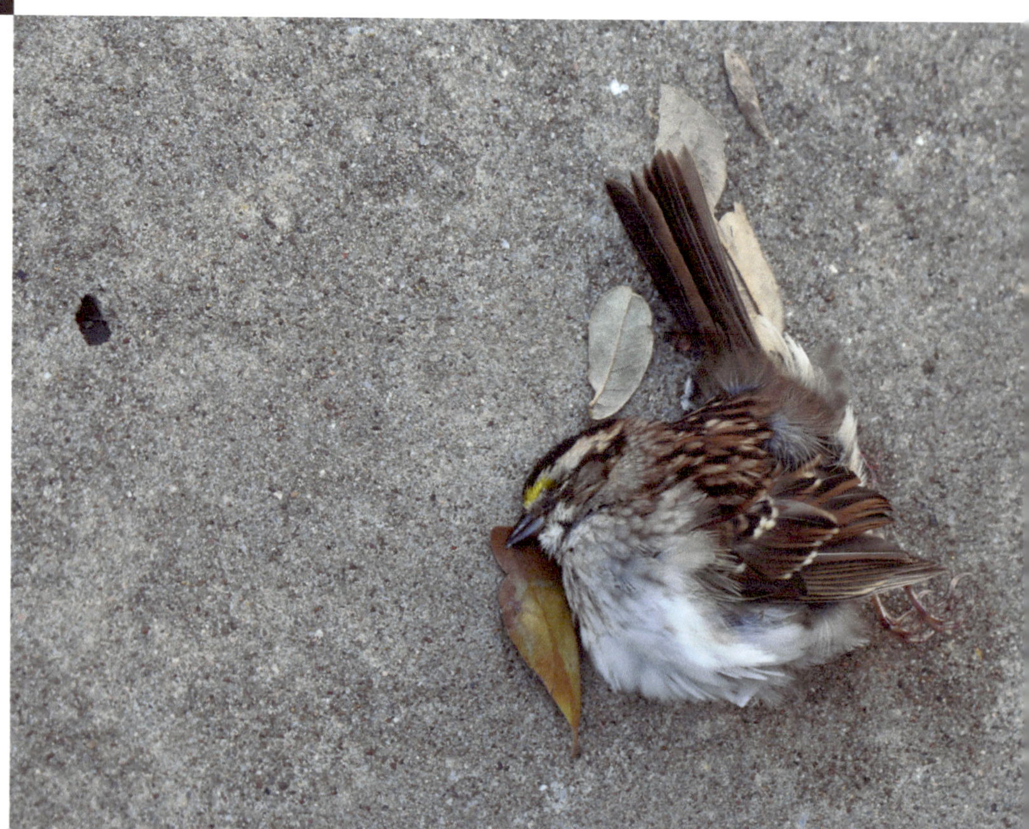

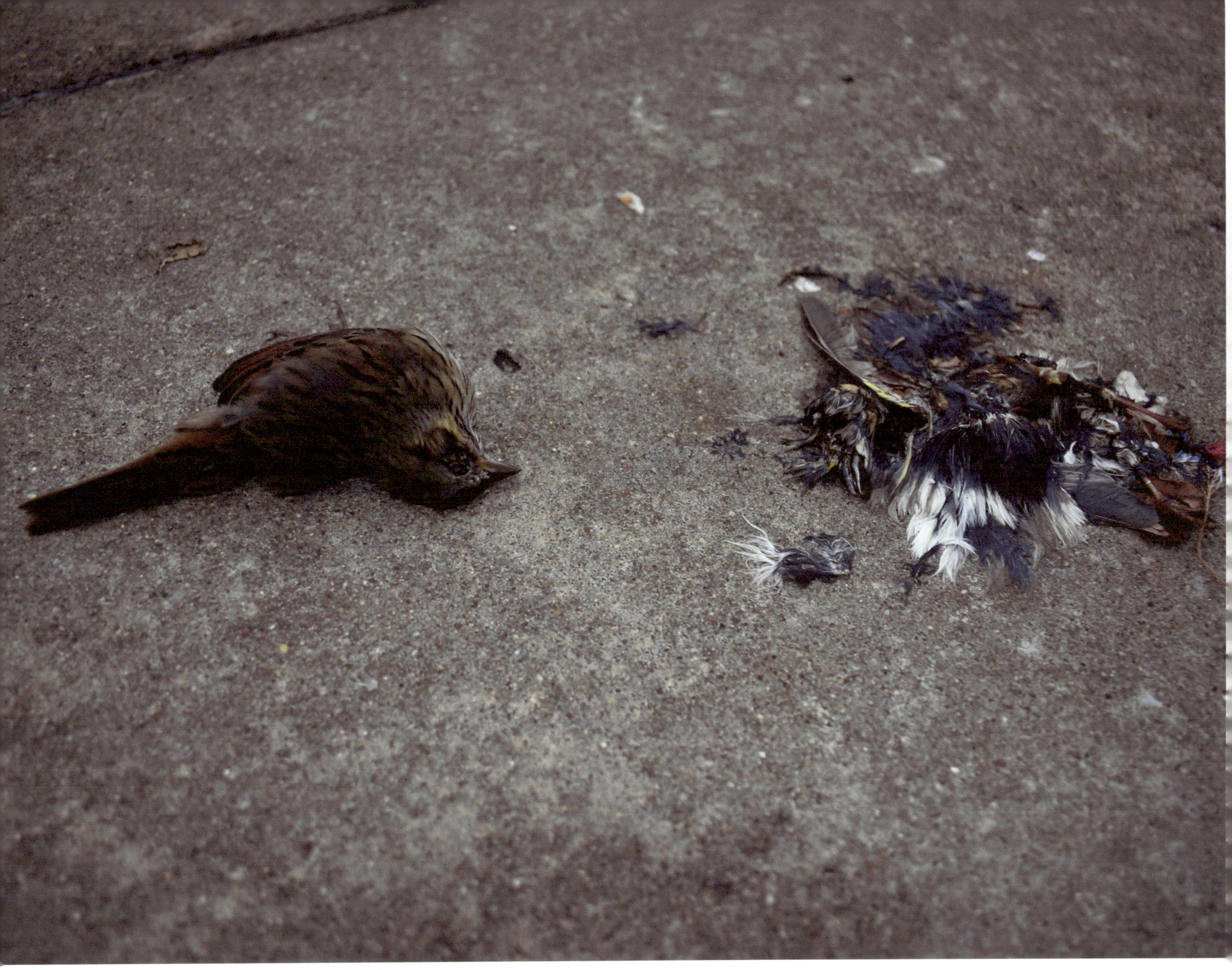

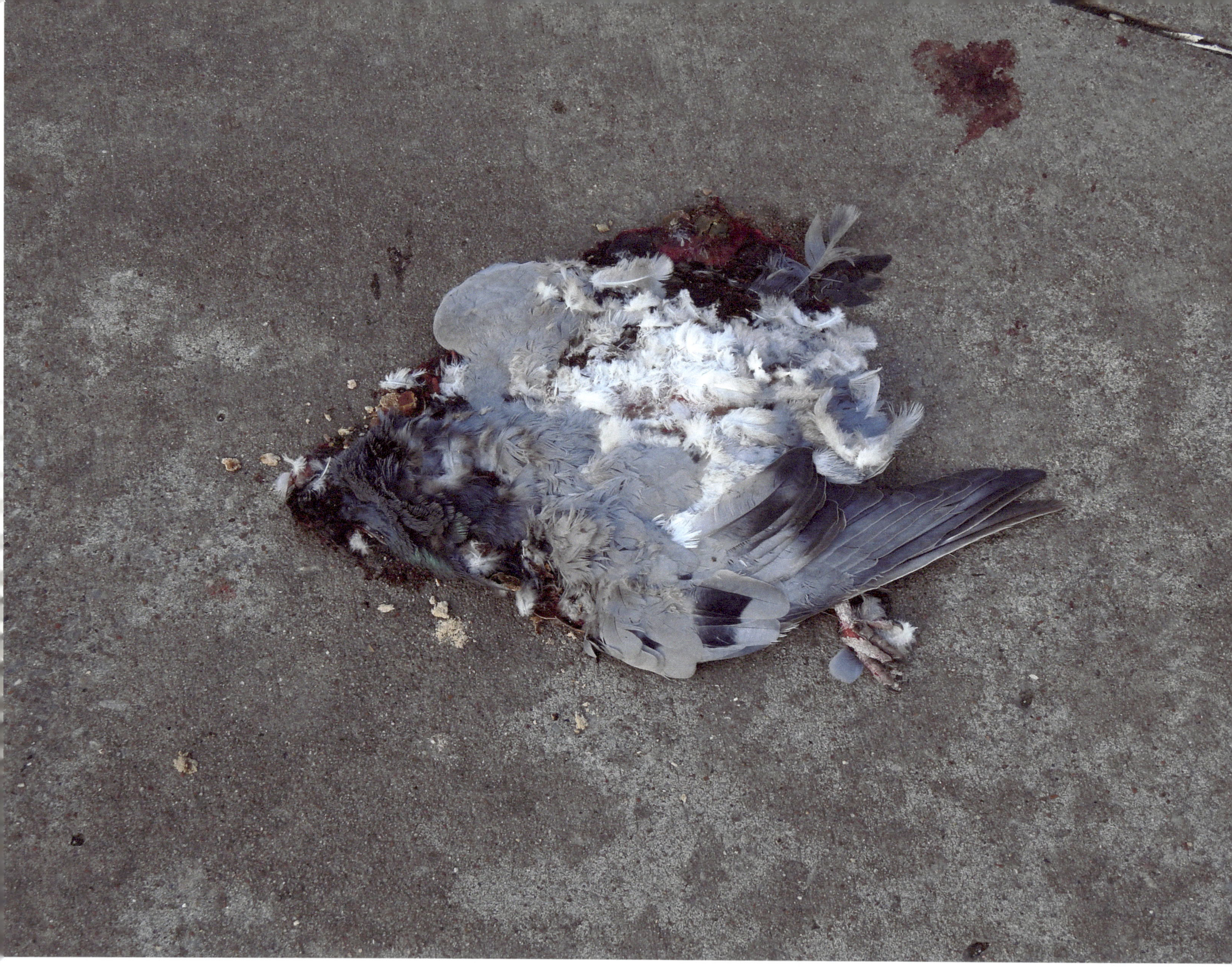

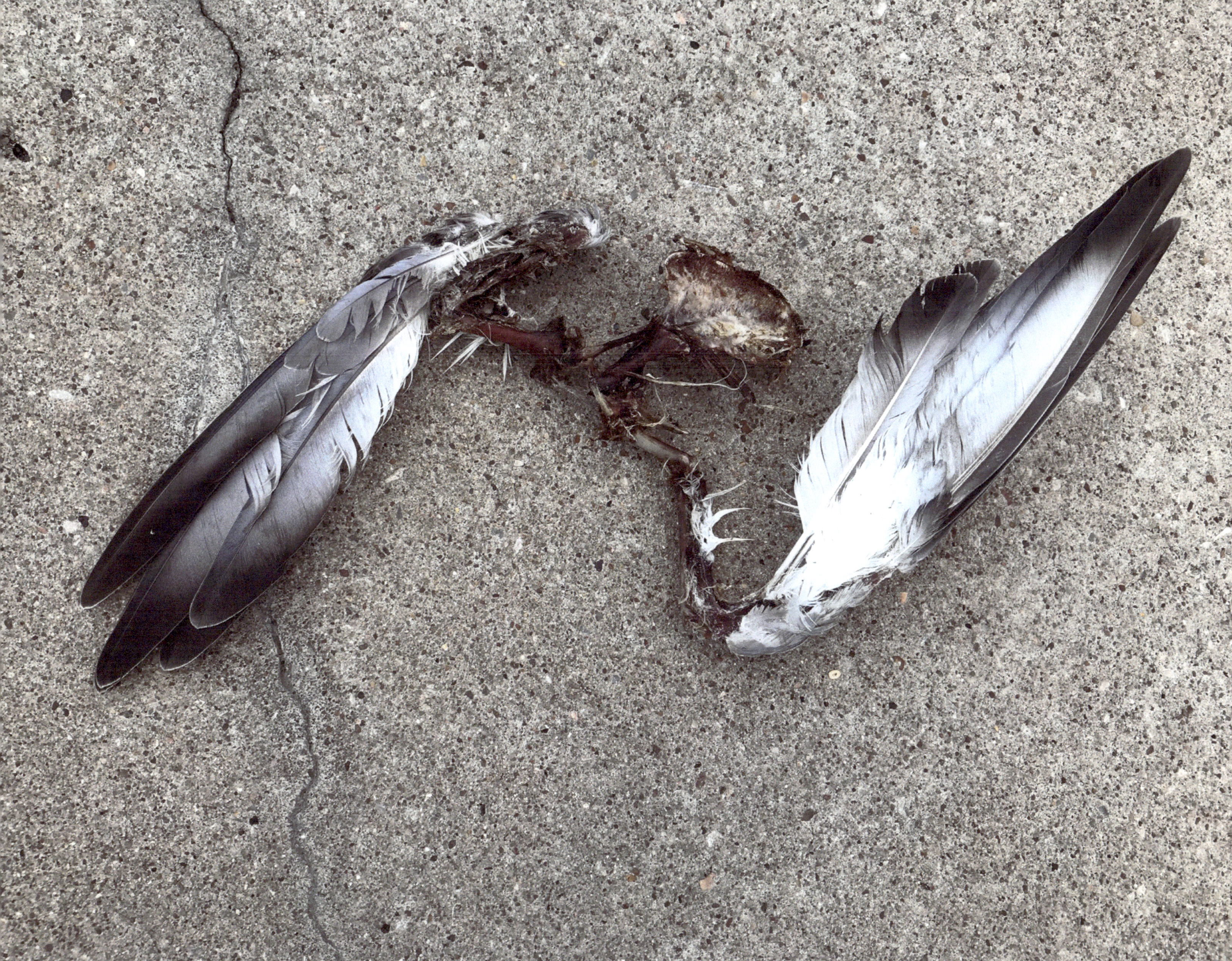

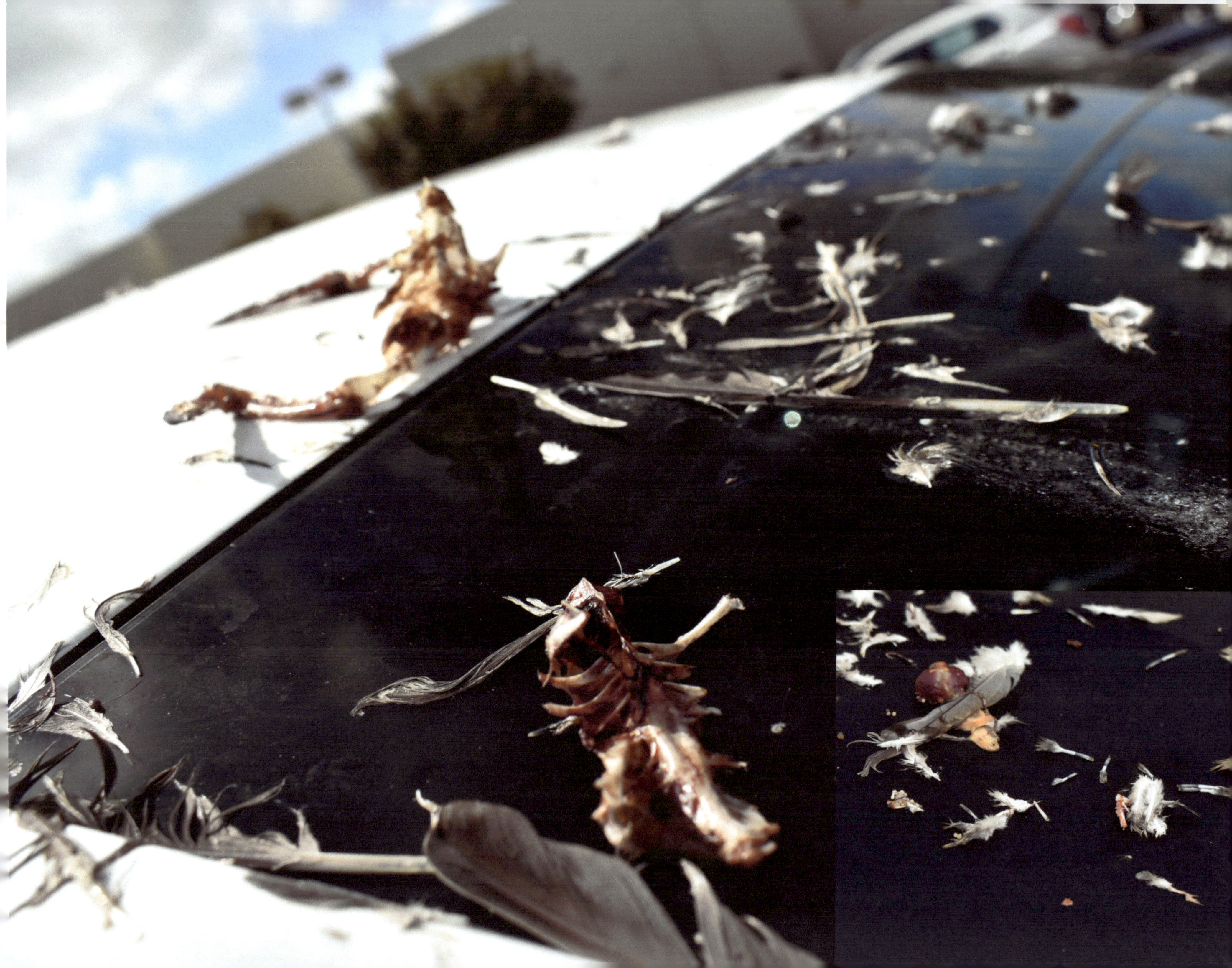

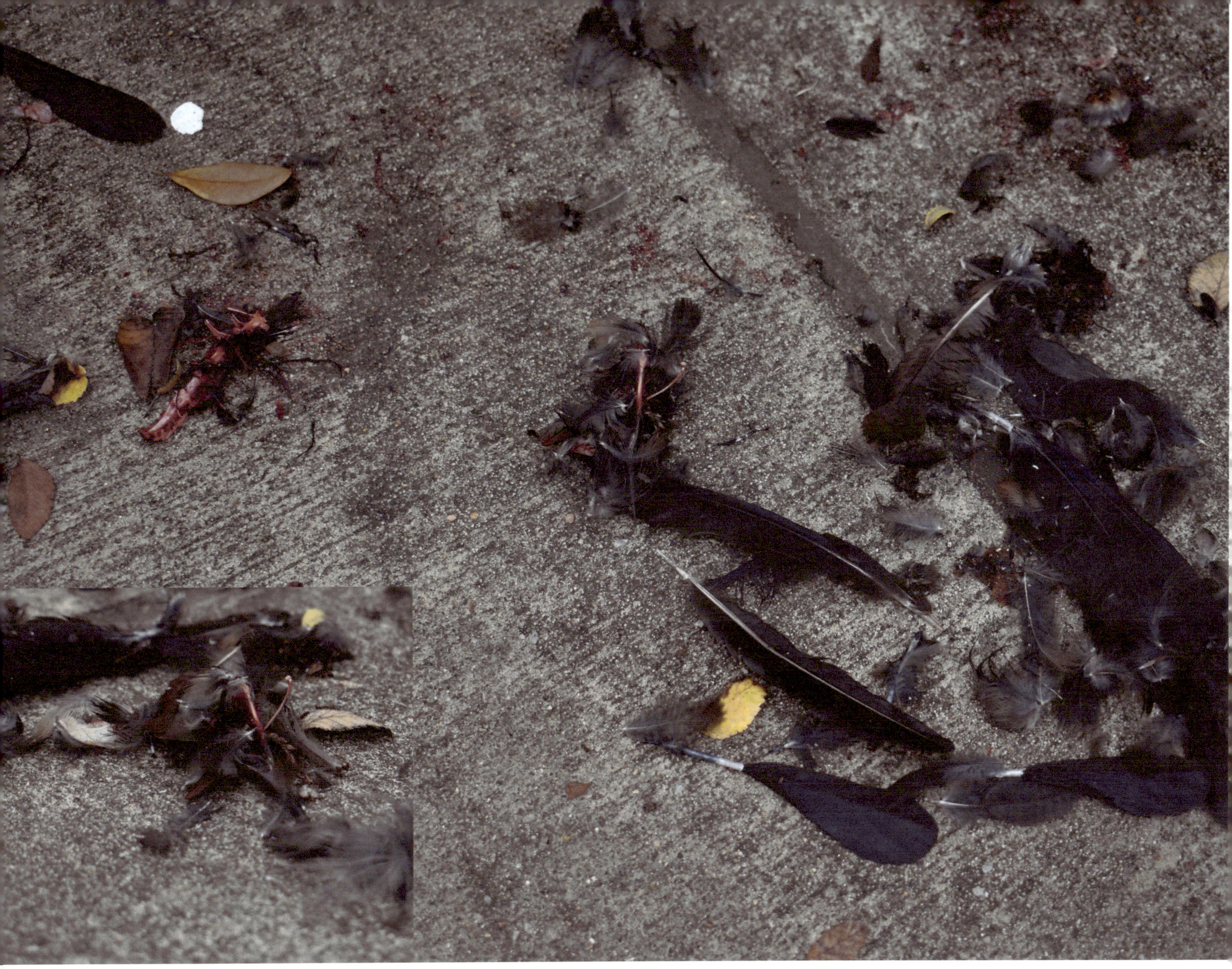

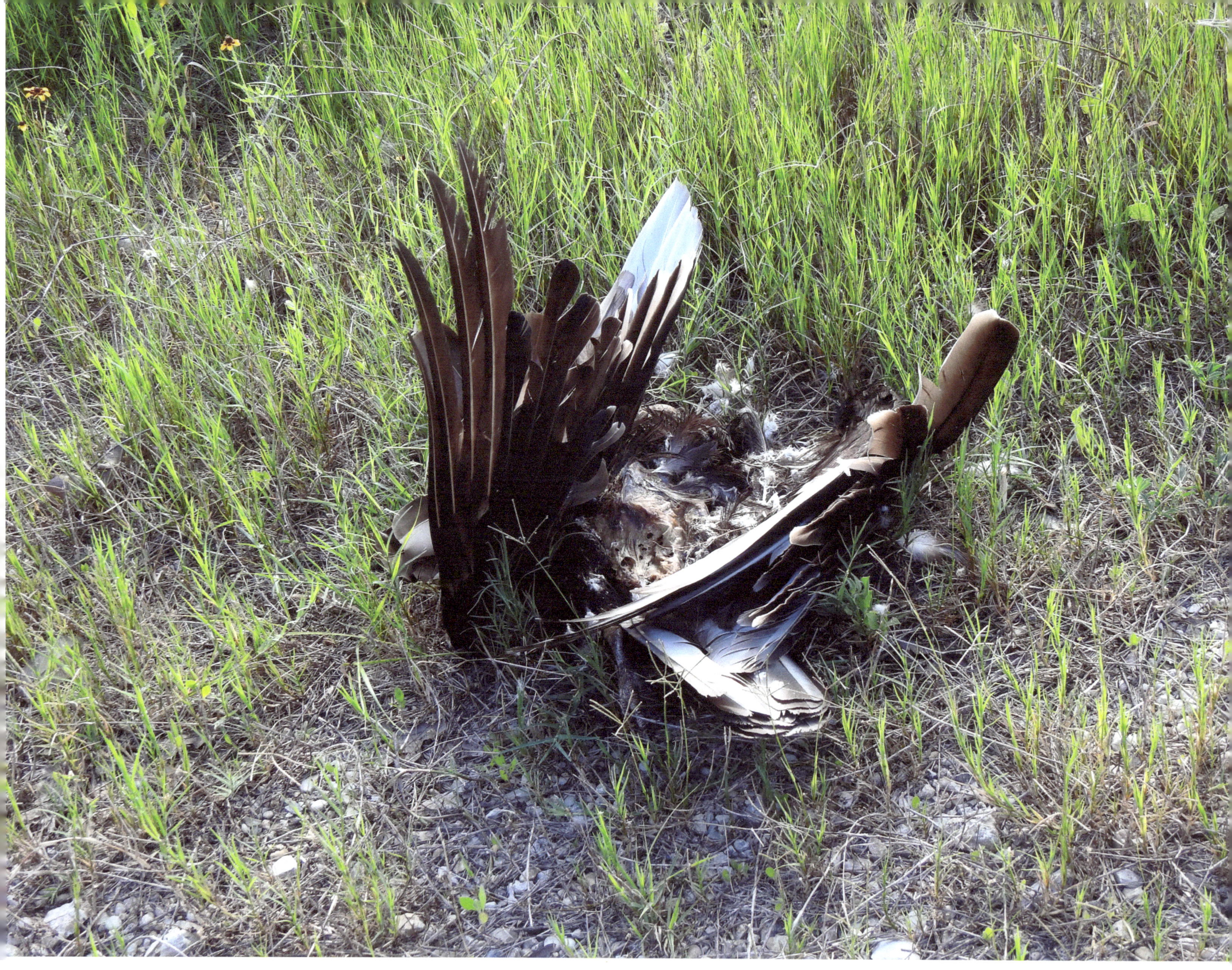

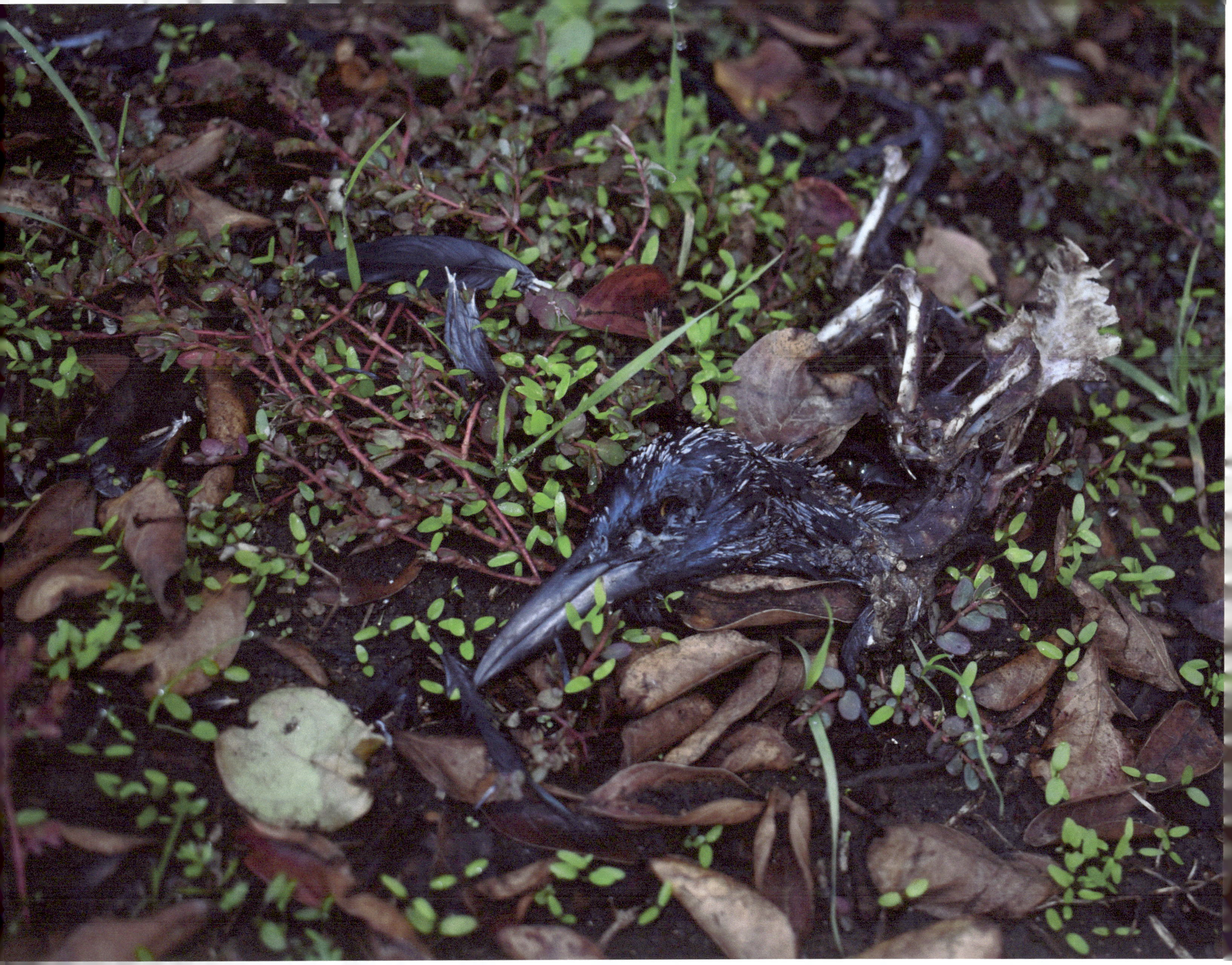

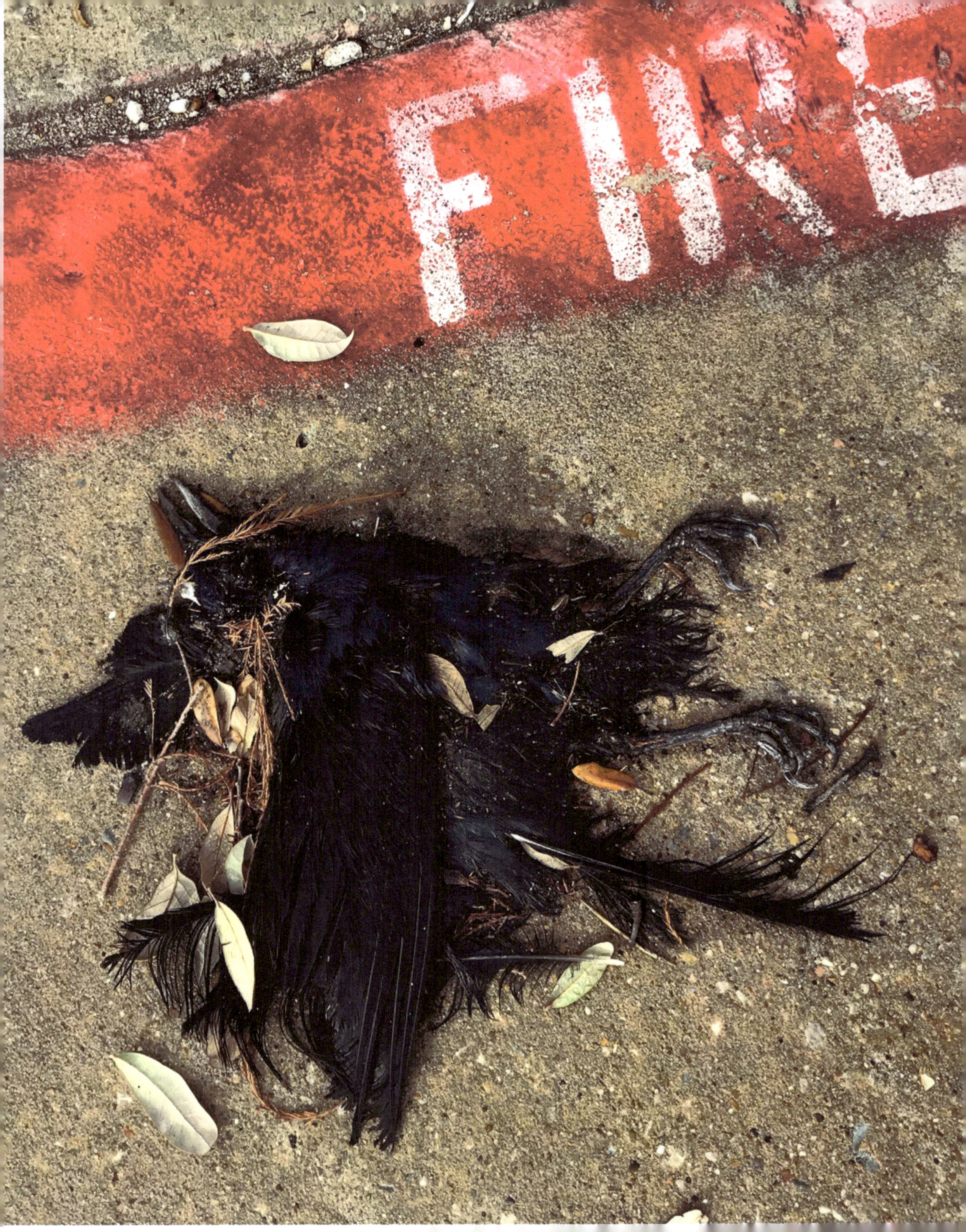
FIRE

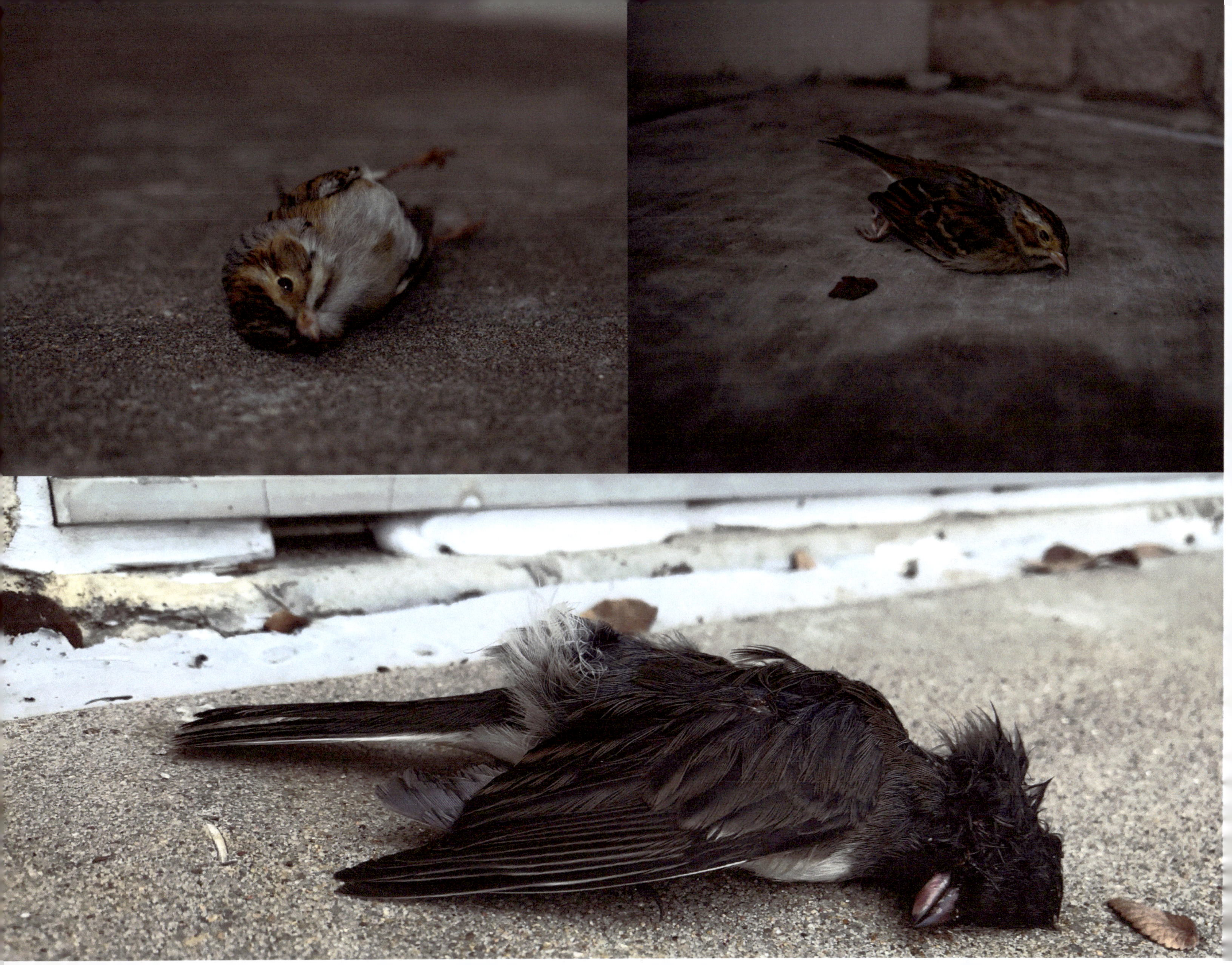

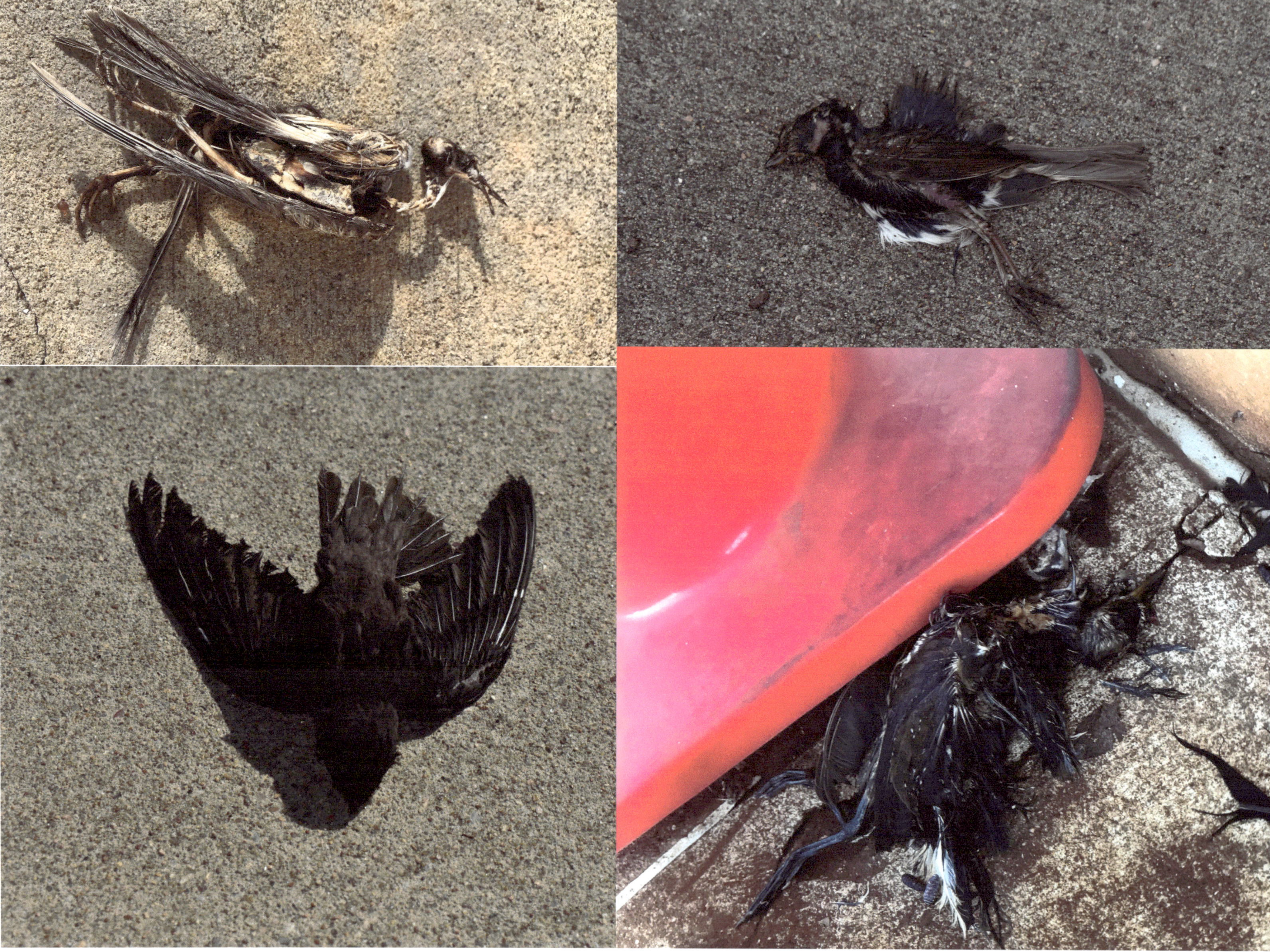

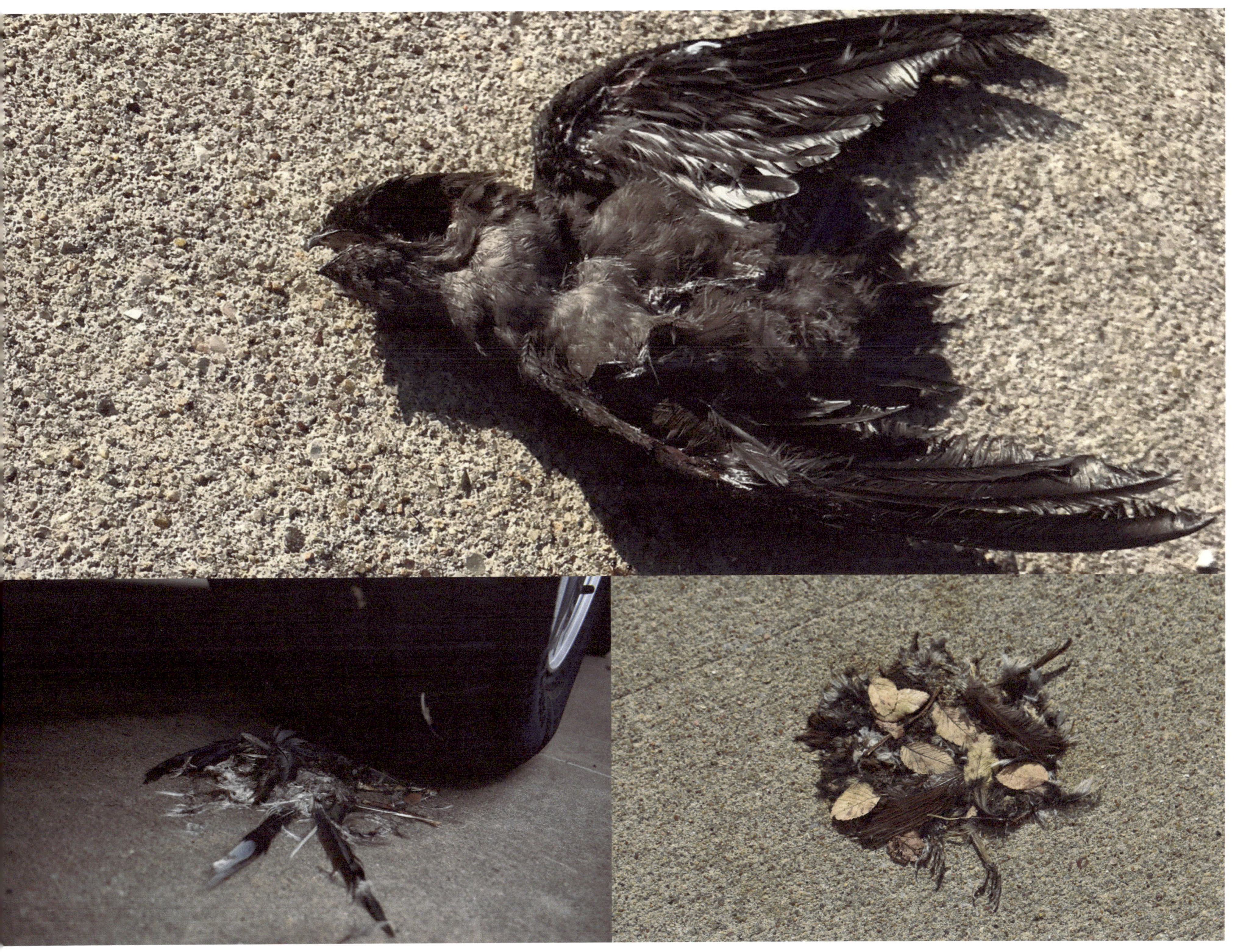

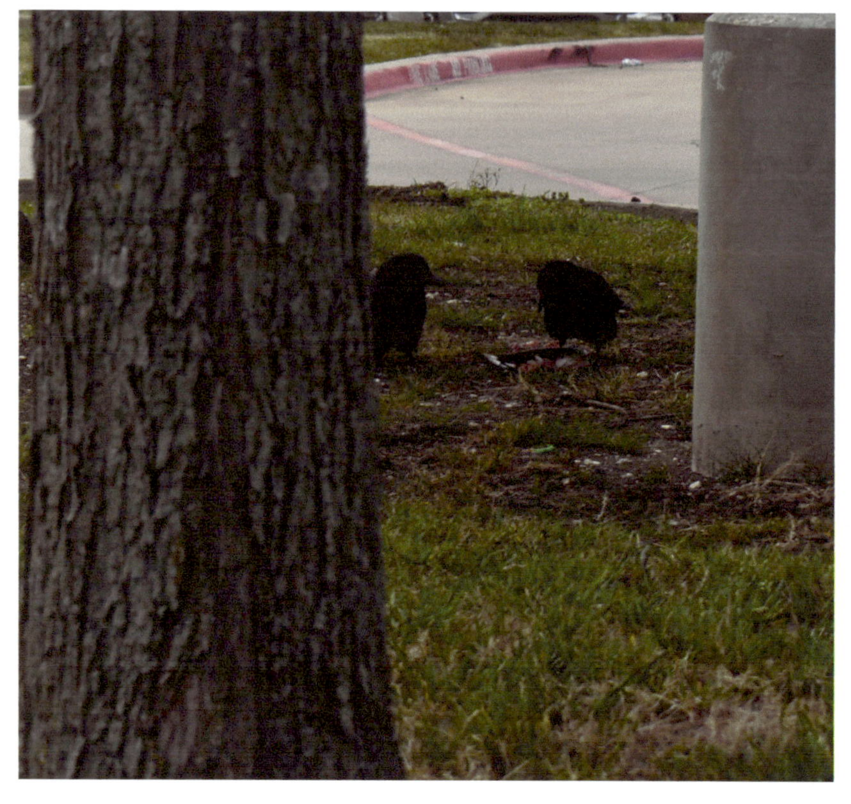
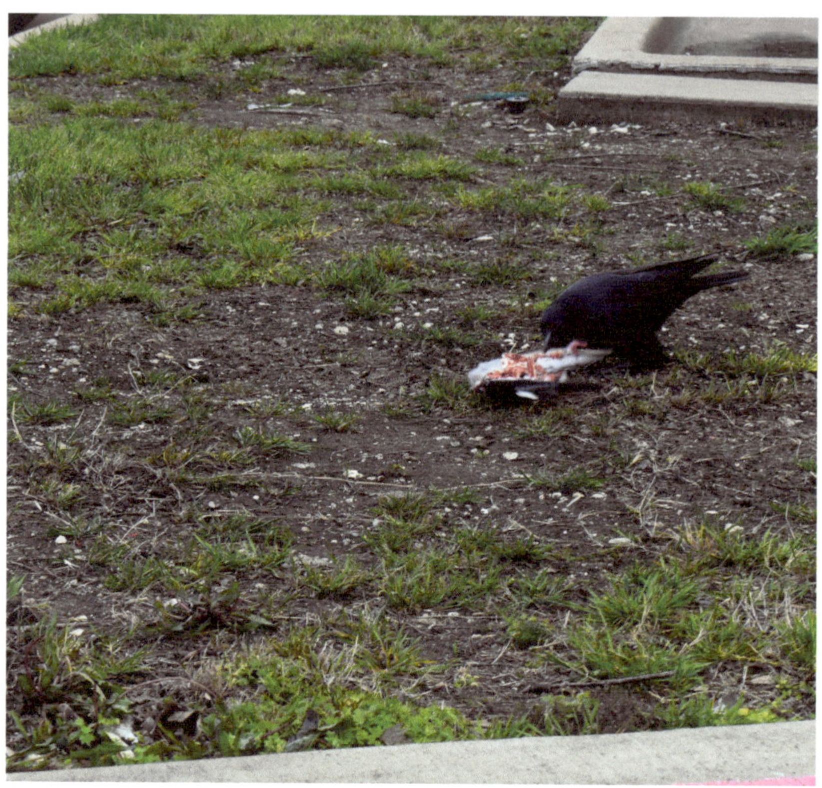
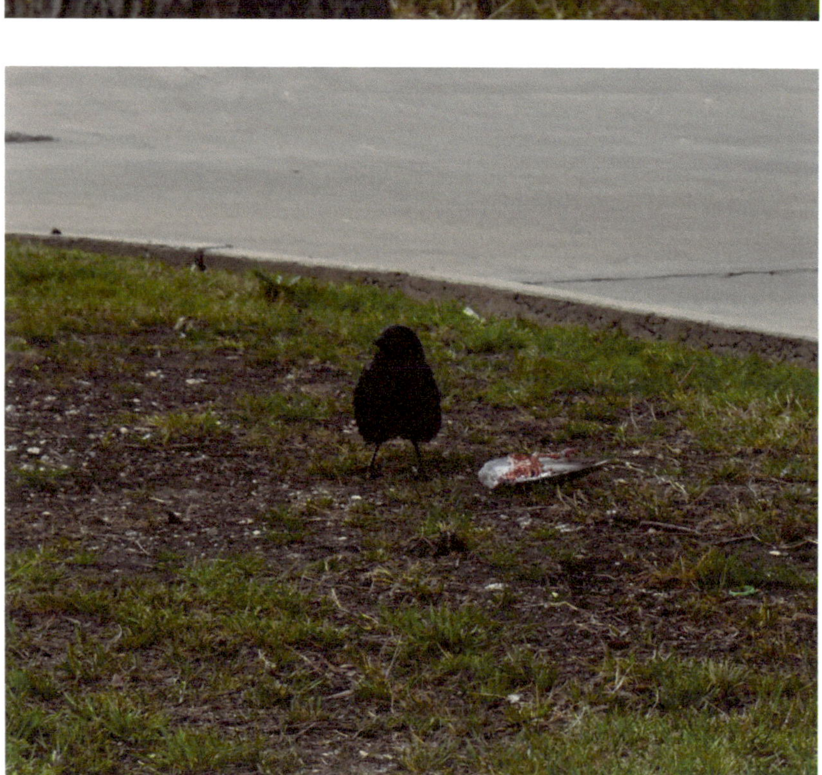
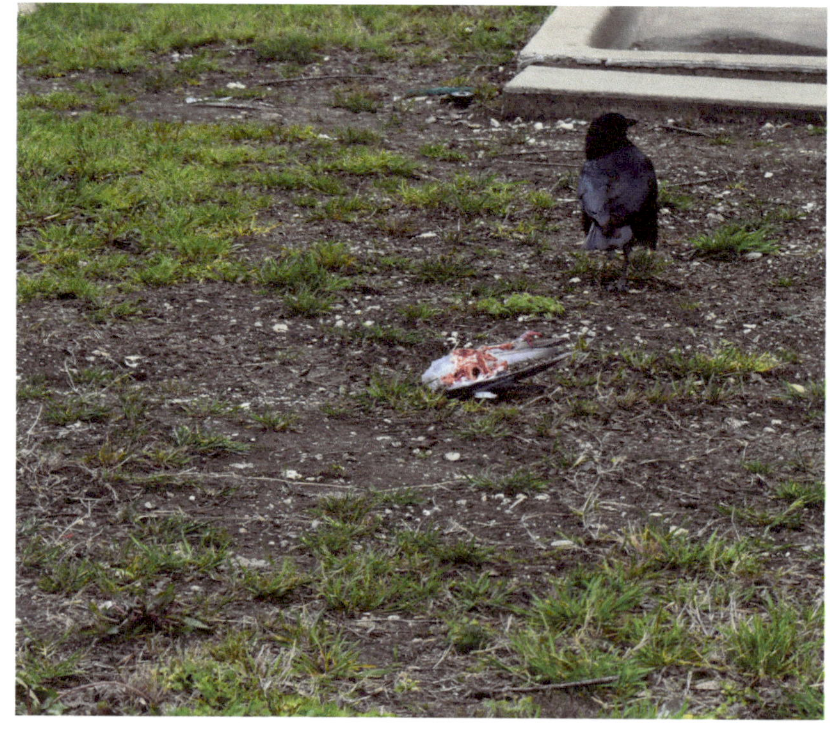

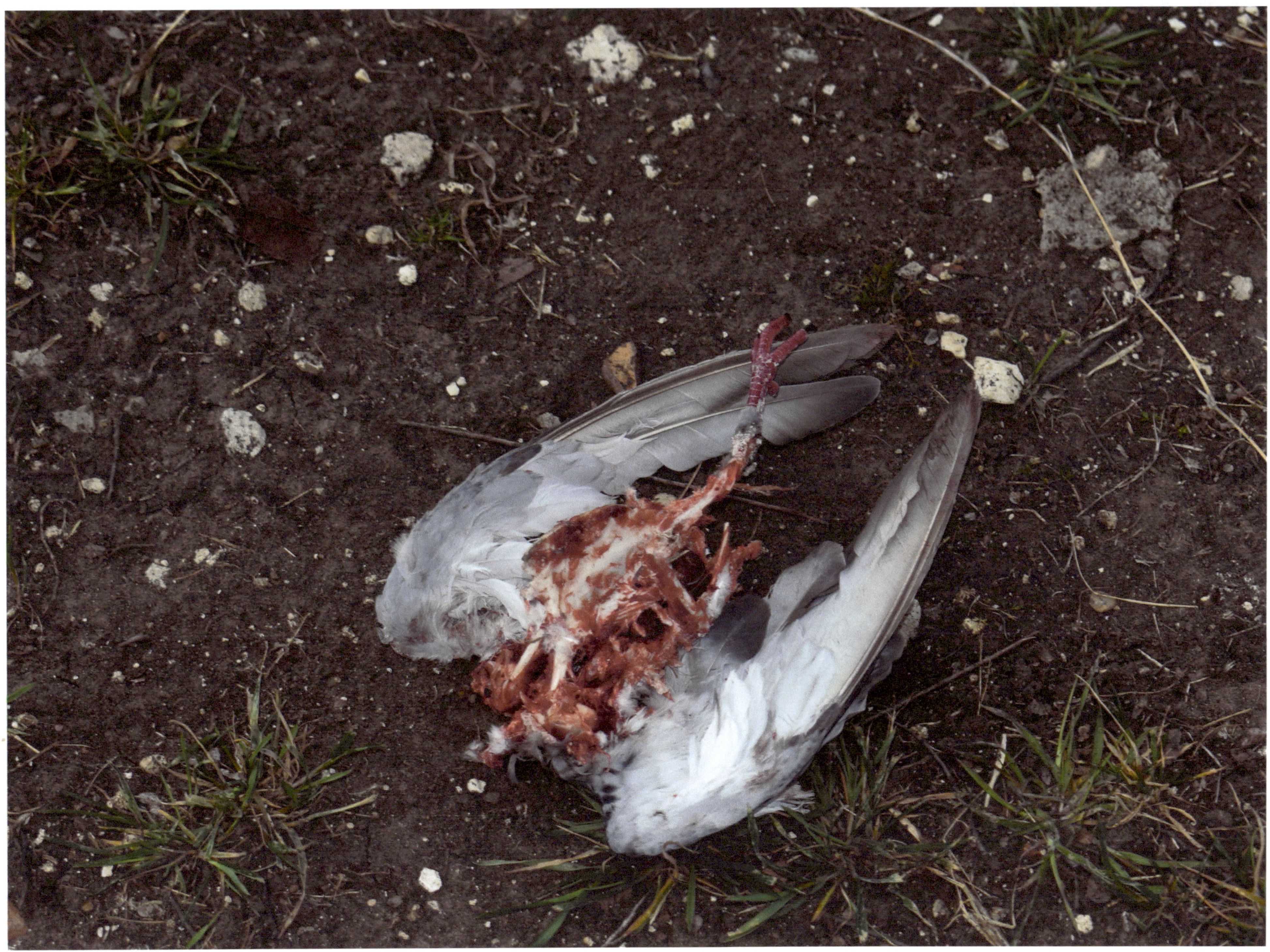

The Funeral of Steve the Grackle

One day I was sitting at my desk and looked outside to see this large, beautiful, dead grackle. His colors shone in the sunlight. I went out to pay my respects and take his picture. I didn't name him Steve until a couple days later when a coworker said, "Someone really needs to deal with that dead bird." I was slightly offended, but I also like to mess with people so I said, "His name is Steve."
Steve is a special case. I had once heard that crows have funerals. It's really more of an investigation than a funeral. Apparently, at least in this case, so do grackles.
I saw Steve outside my window, took my photograph of him, and then set about the rest of my day. I work outside (hence seeing all the dead animals in the first place) and as I was coming back around to where my office is I saw several birds had gathered around Steve, and then more gathered. Later when I was coming inside I noticed Steve had been moved. I was able to tell because Steve had a head wound, and was now separate from where he had bled out.
The next morning I came in my office, Steve was still right outside my window. I set my stuff down and was blown away by what I was seeing. Tons of birds had gathered outside my window. One bird was on top of Steve, I believe trying to carry him away.

I feel truly honored to have witnessed something that most people wouldn't have thought twice about.
So I dedicated this book to Steve.

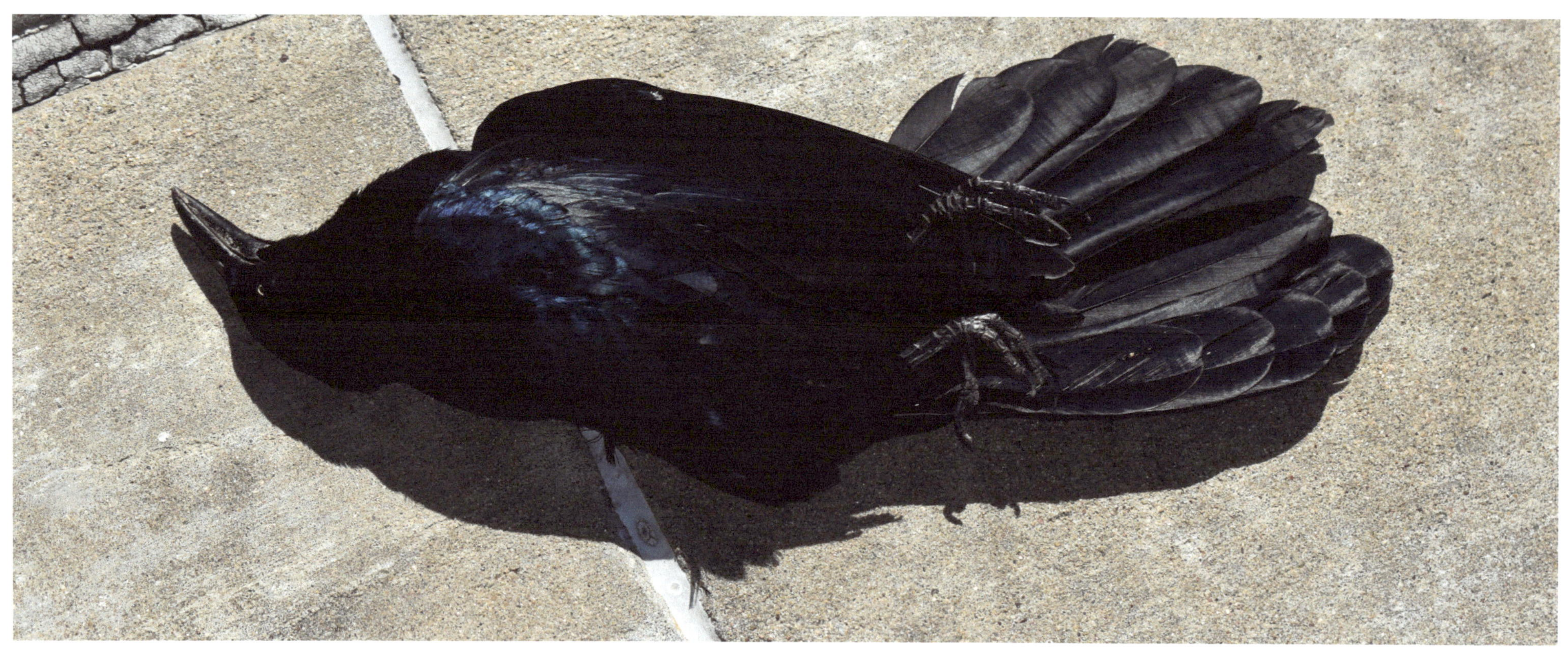

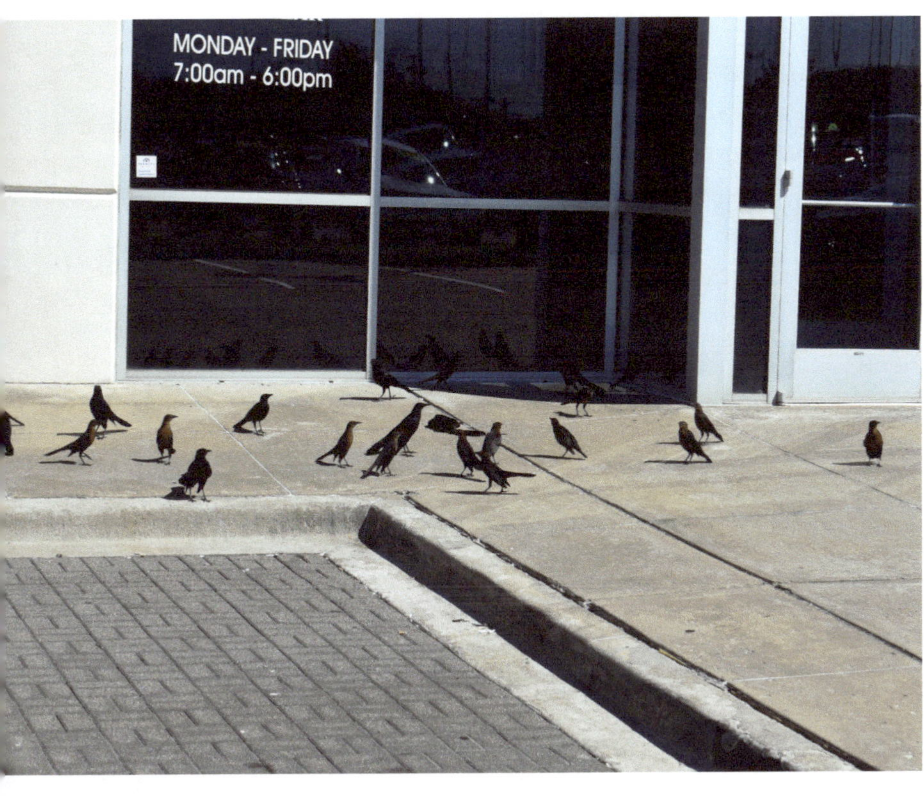

MONDAY - FRIDAY
7:00am - 6:00pm

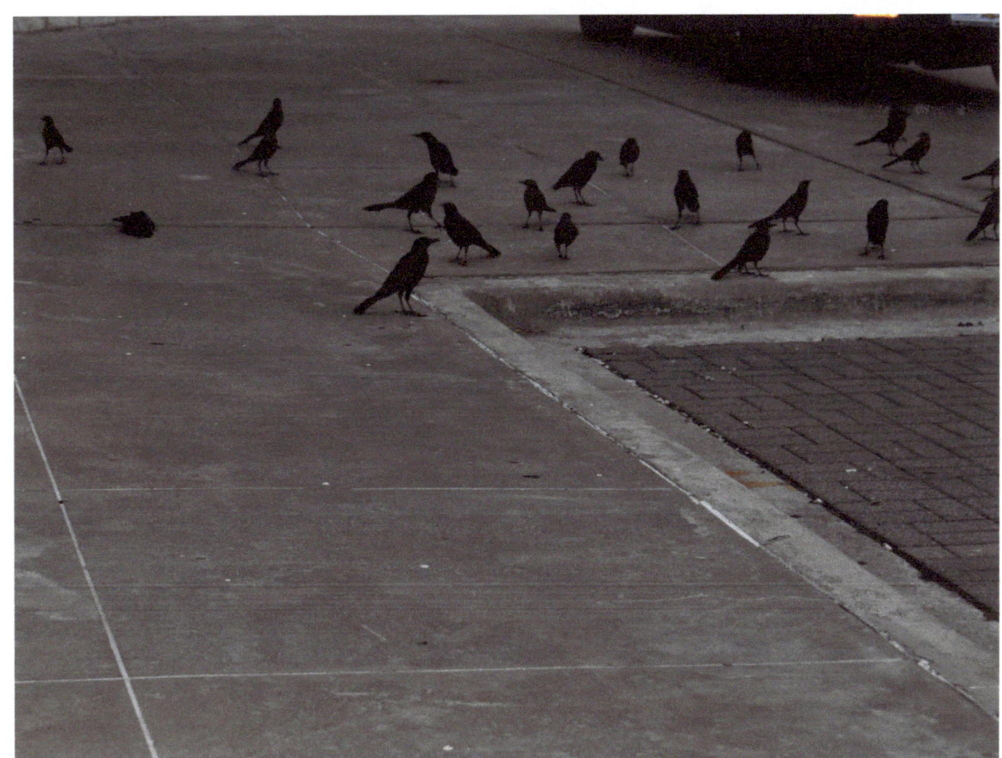
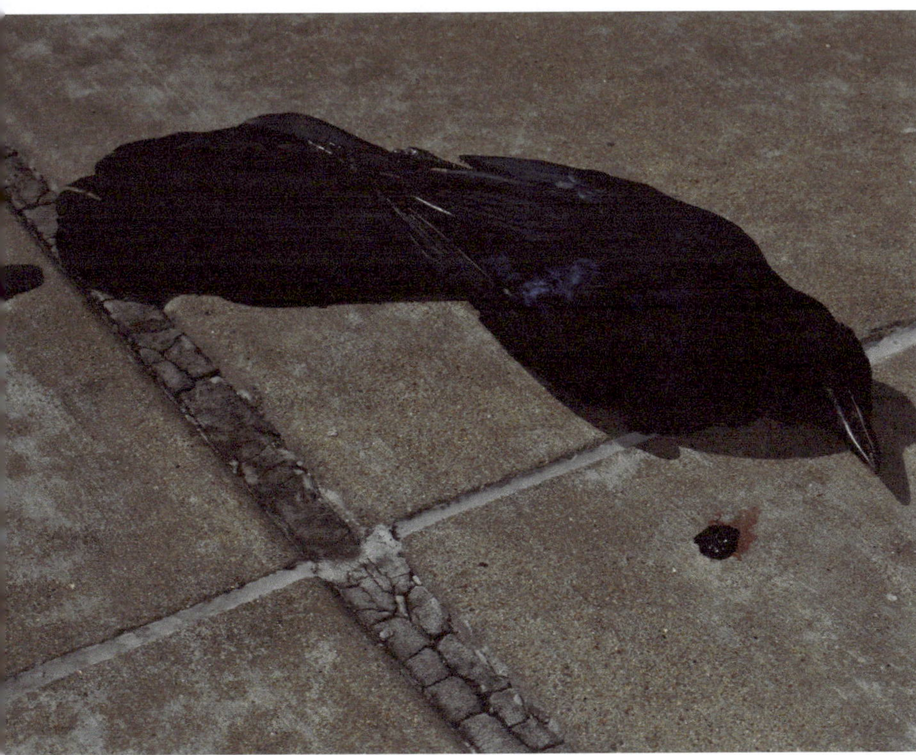
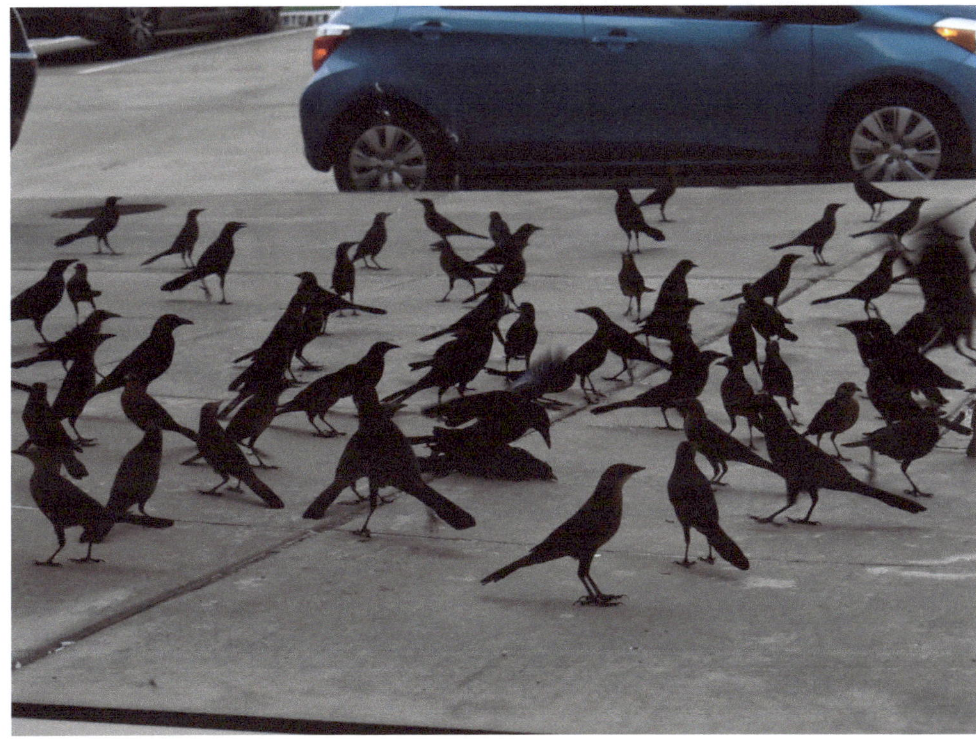

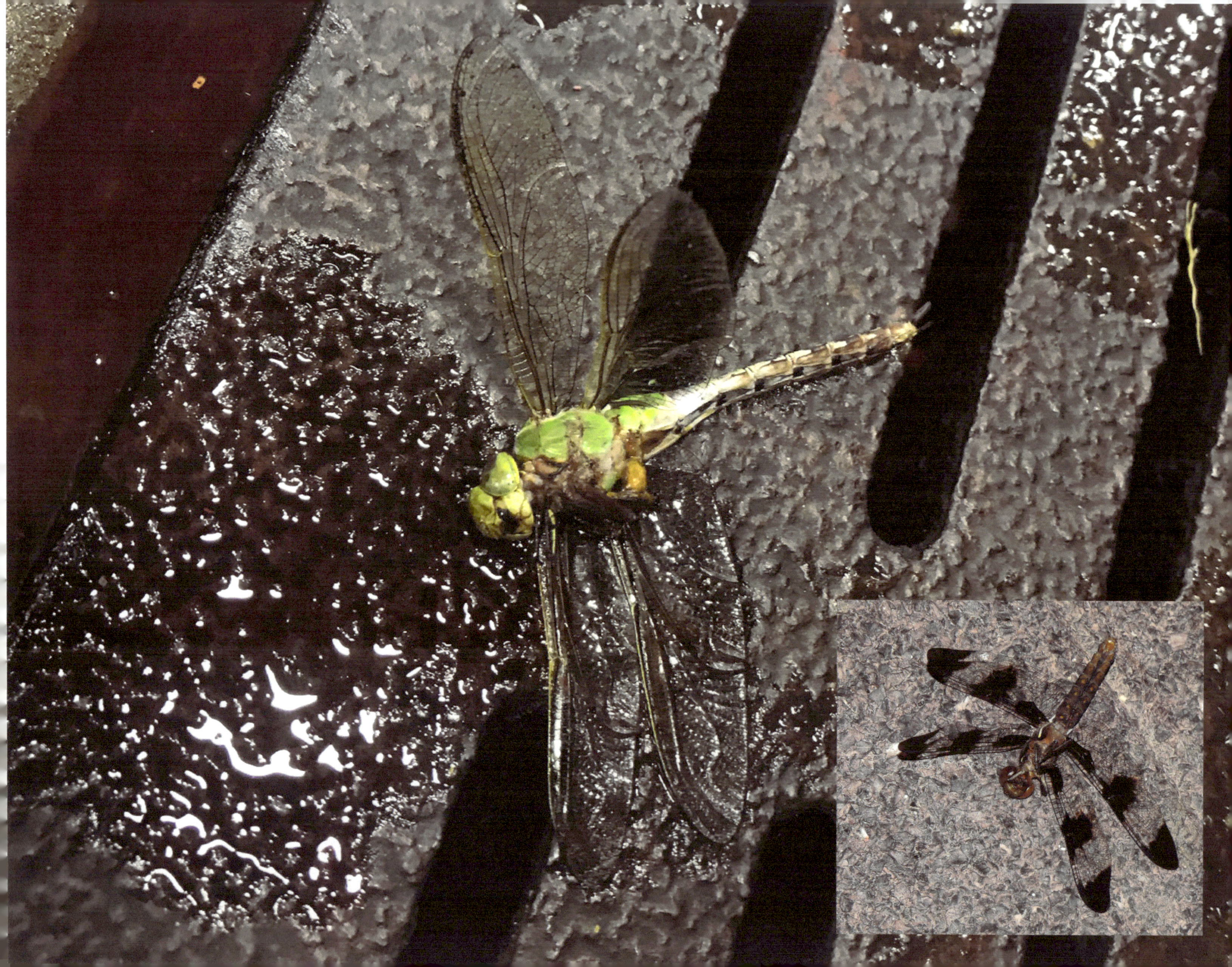

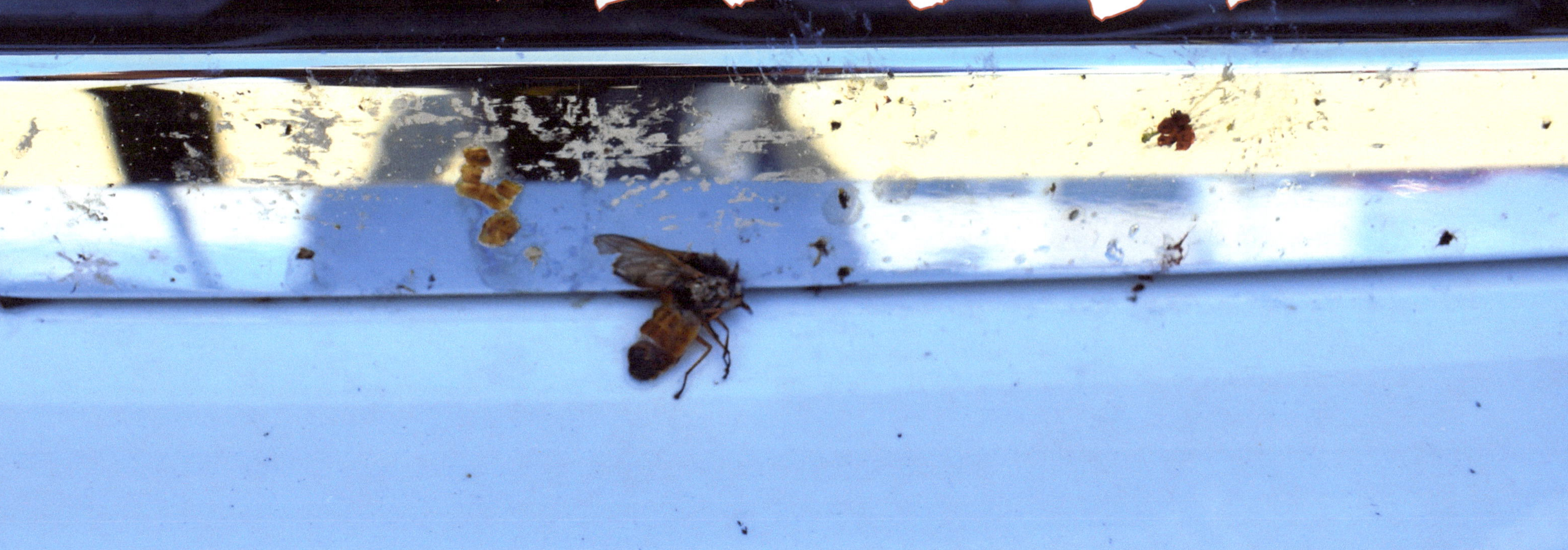

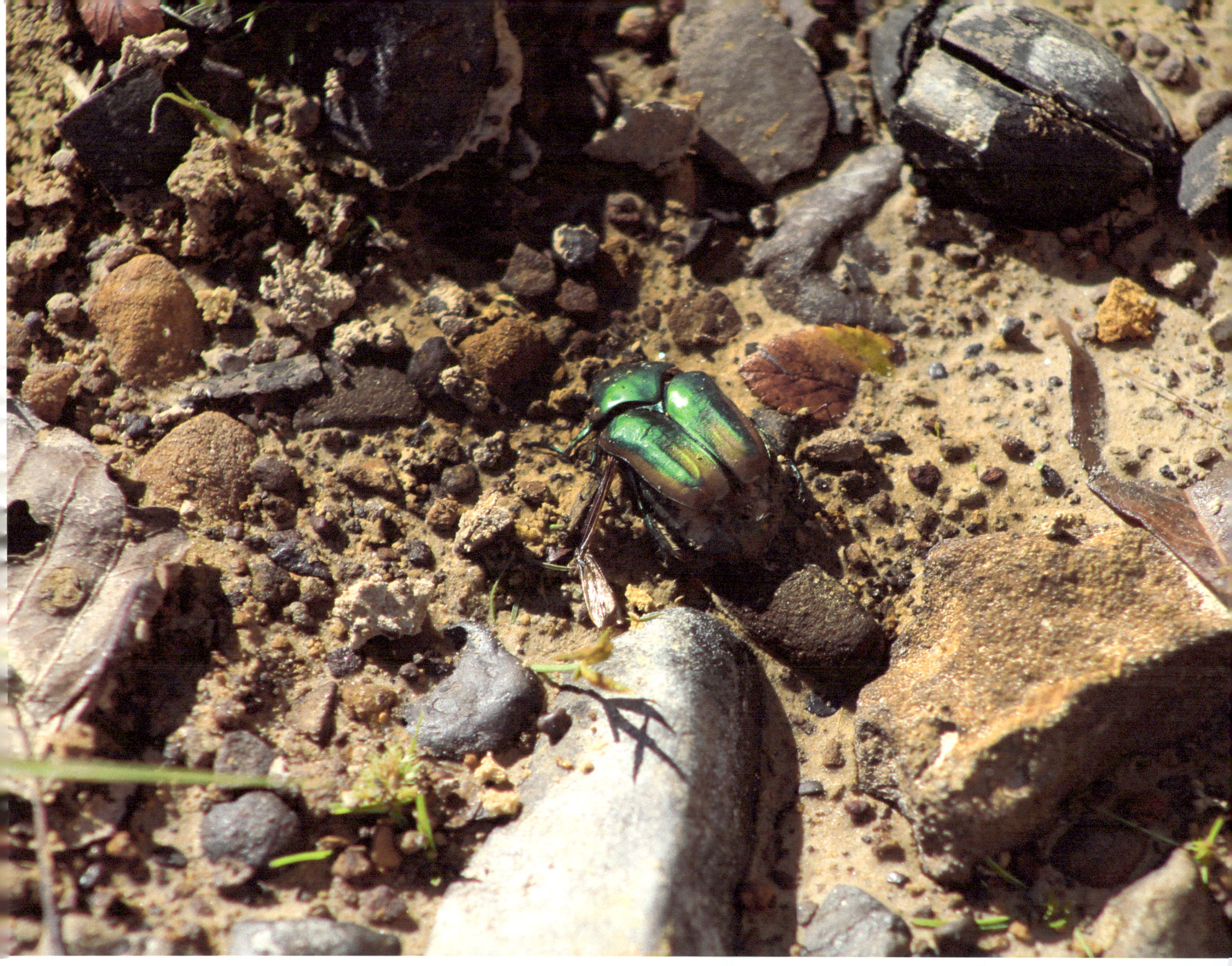

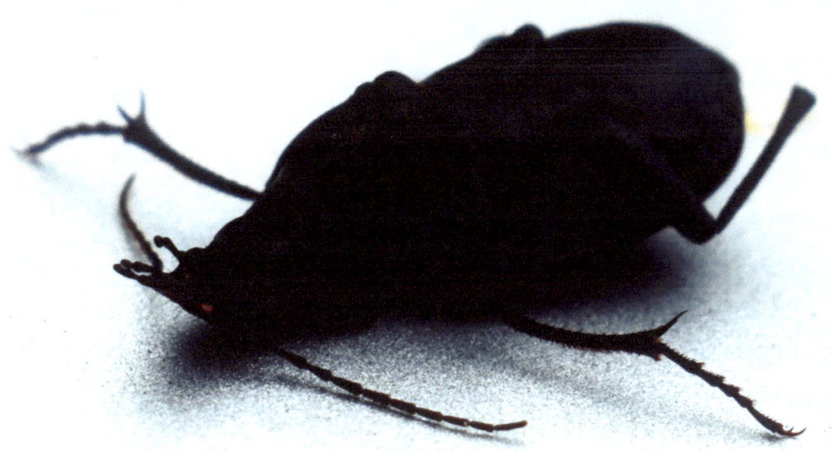

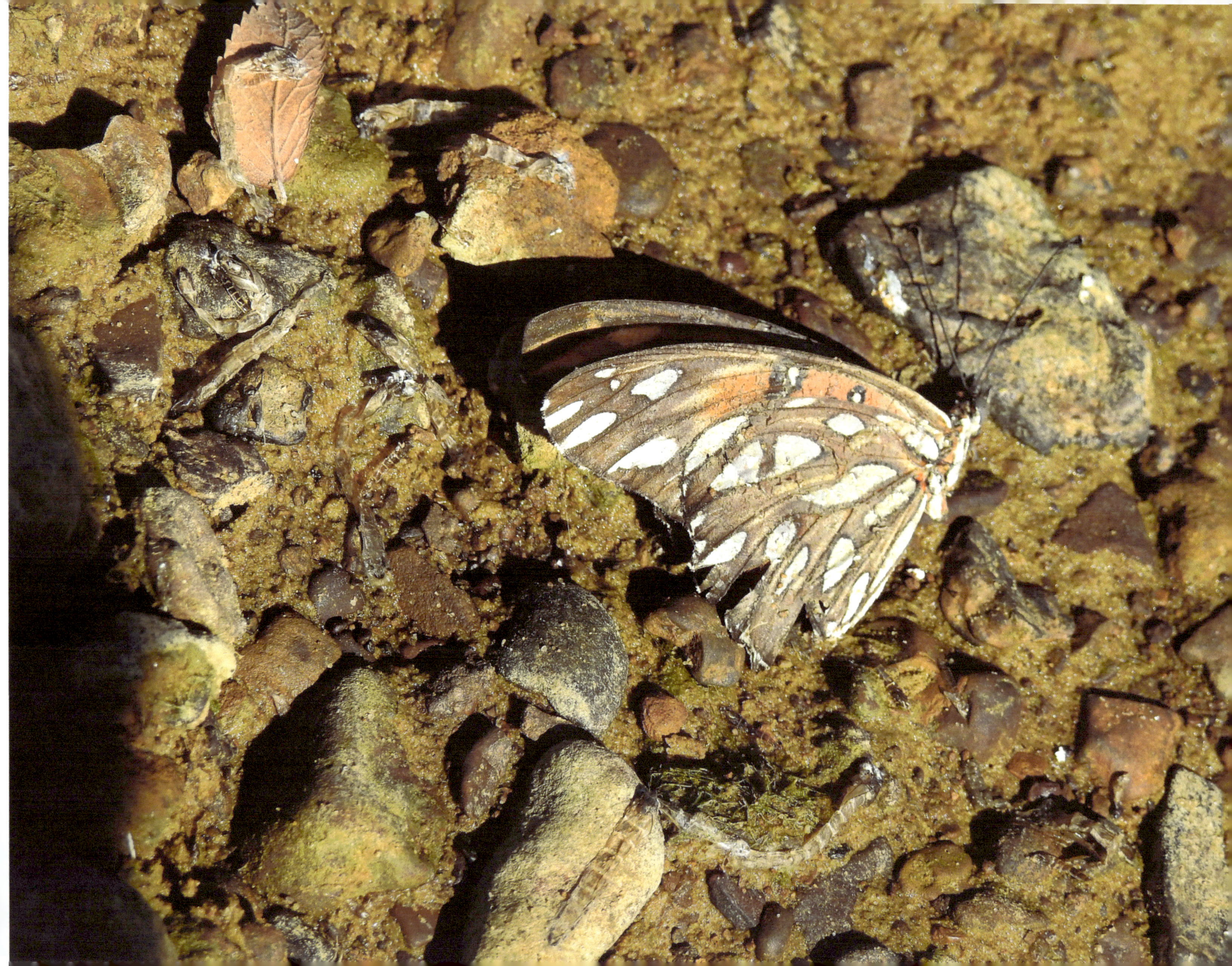

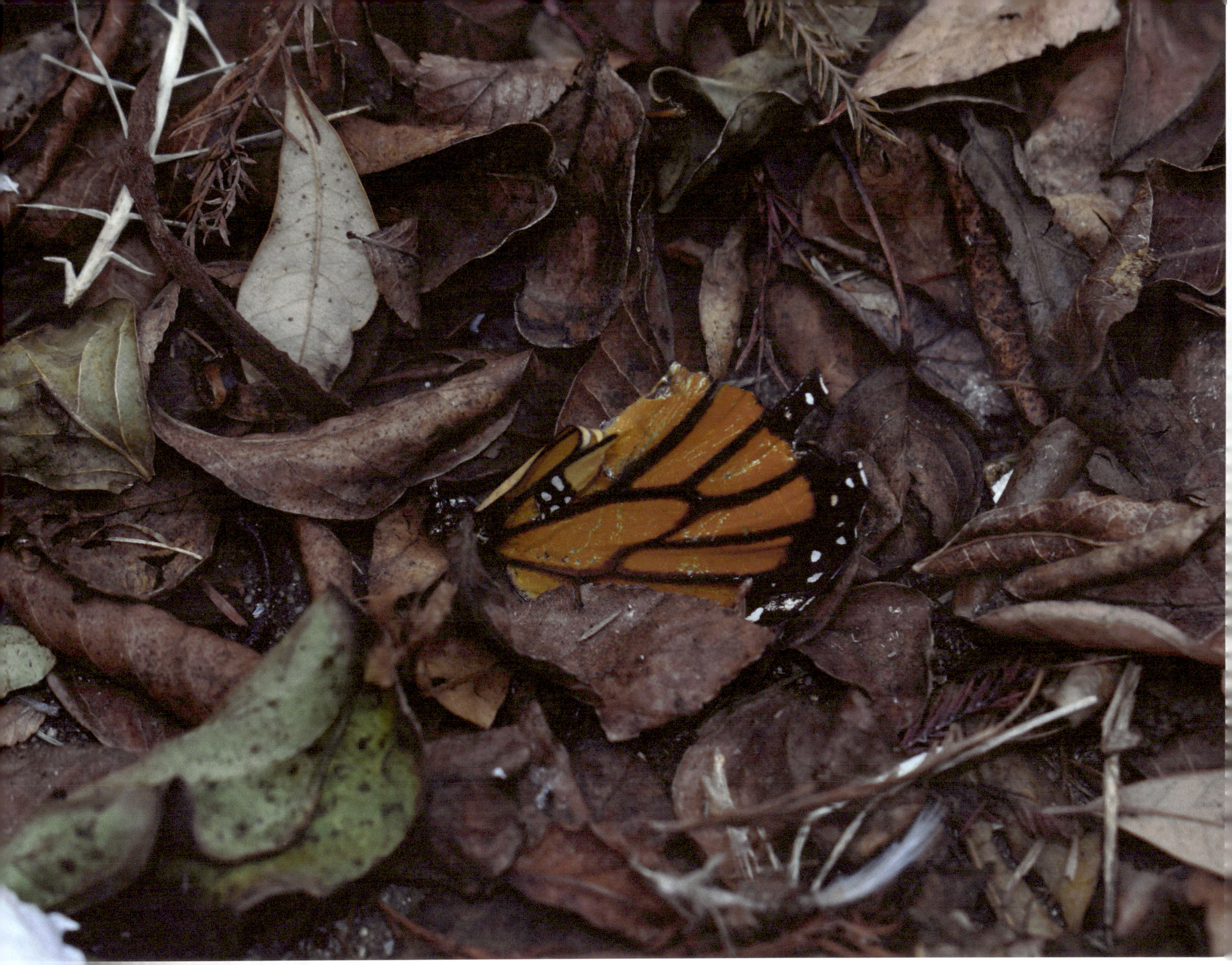

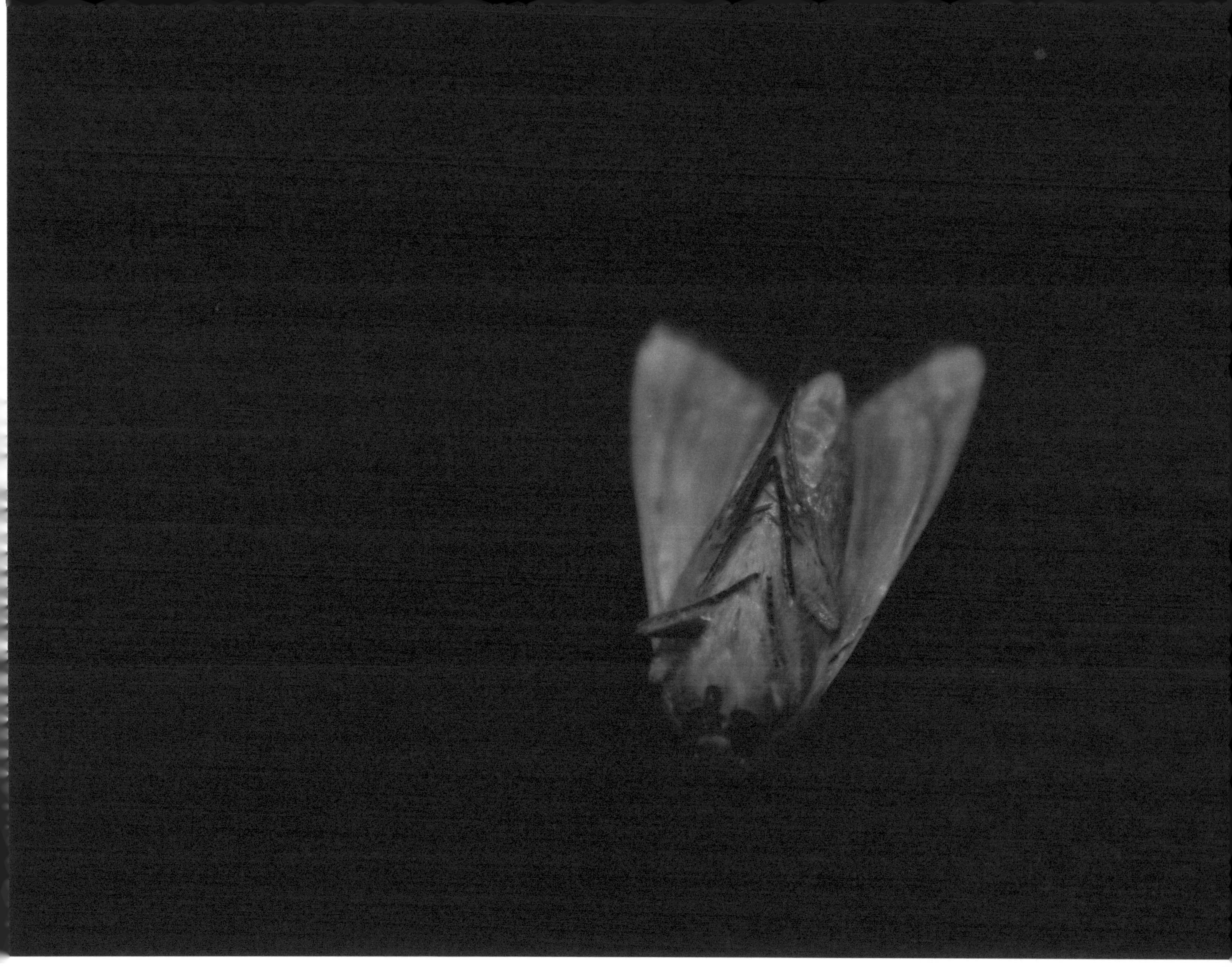

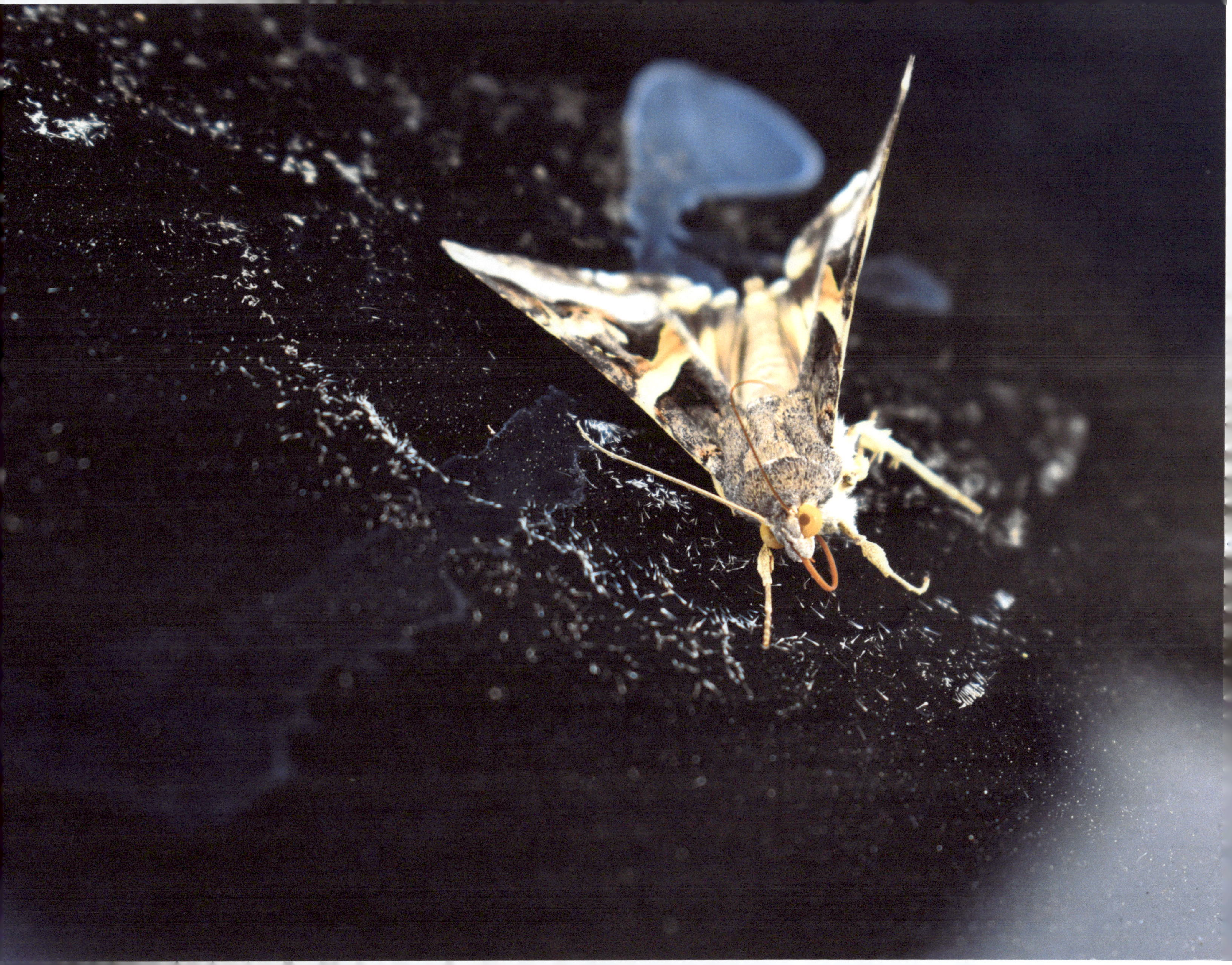

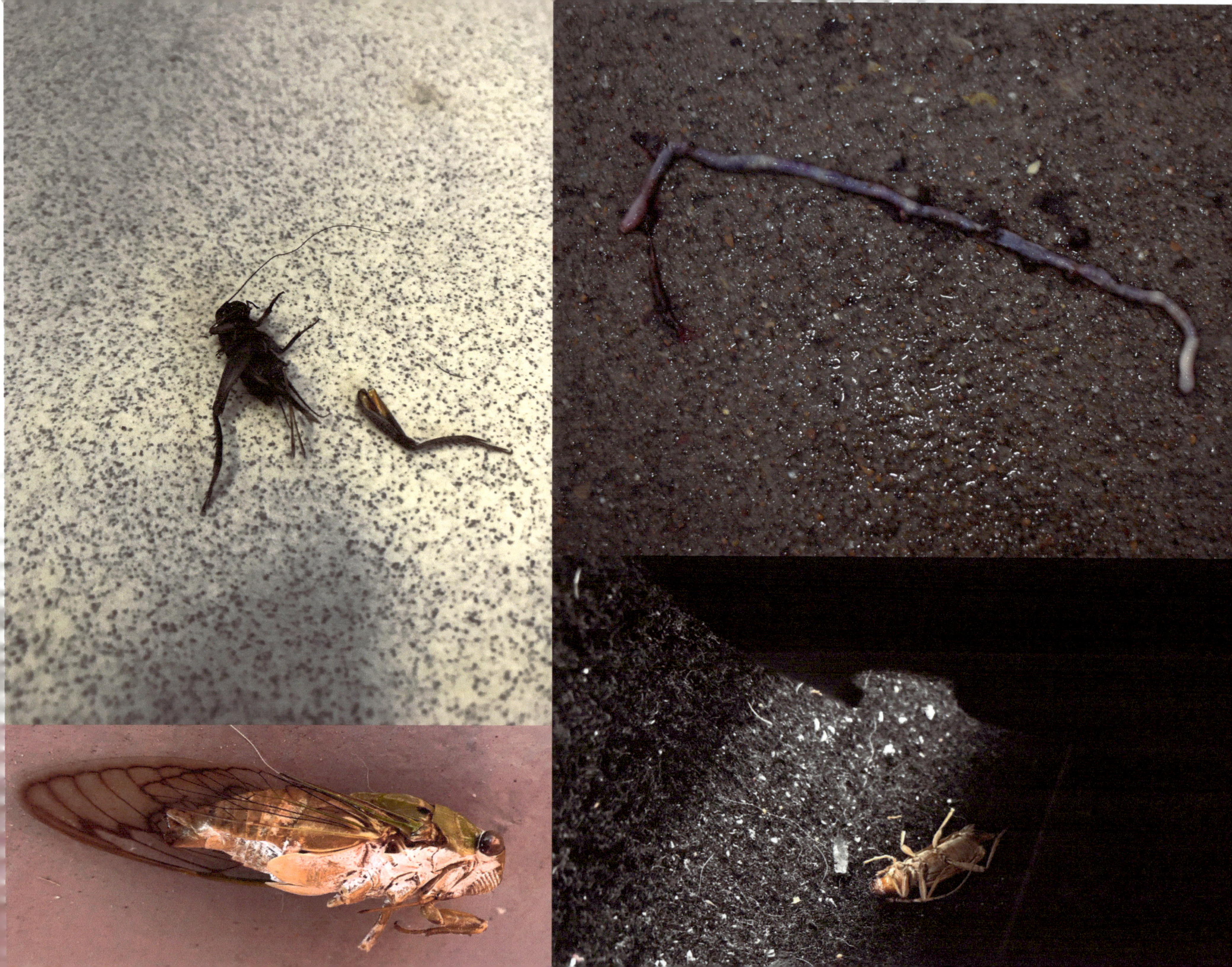

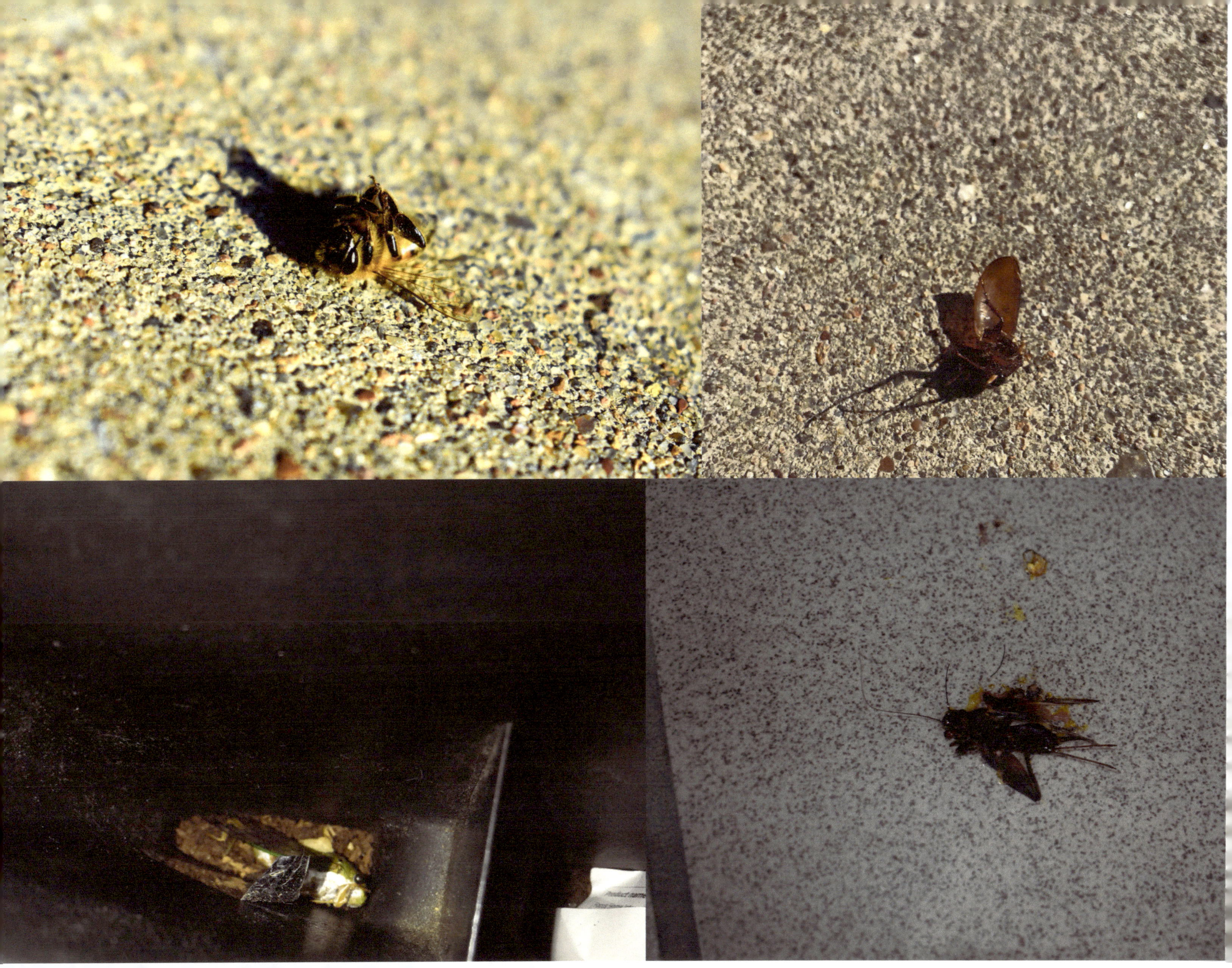

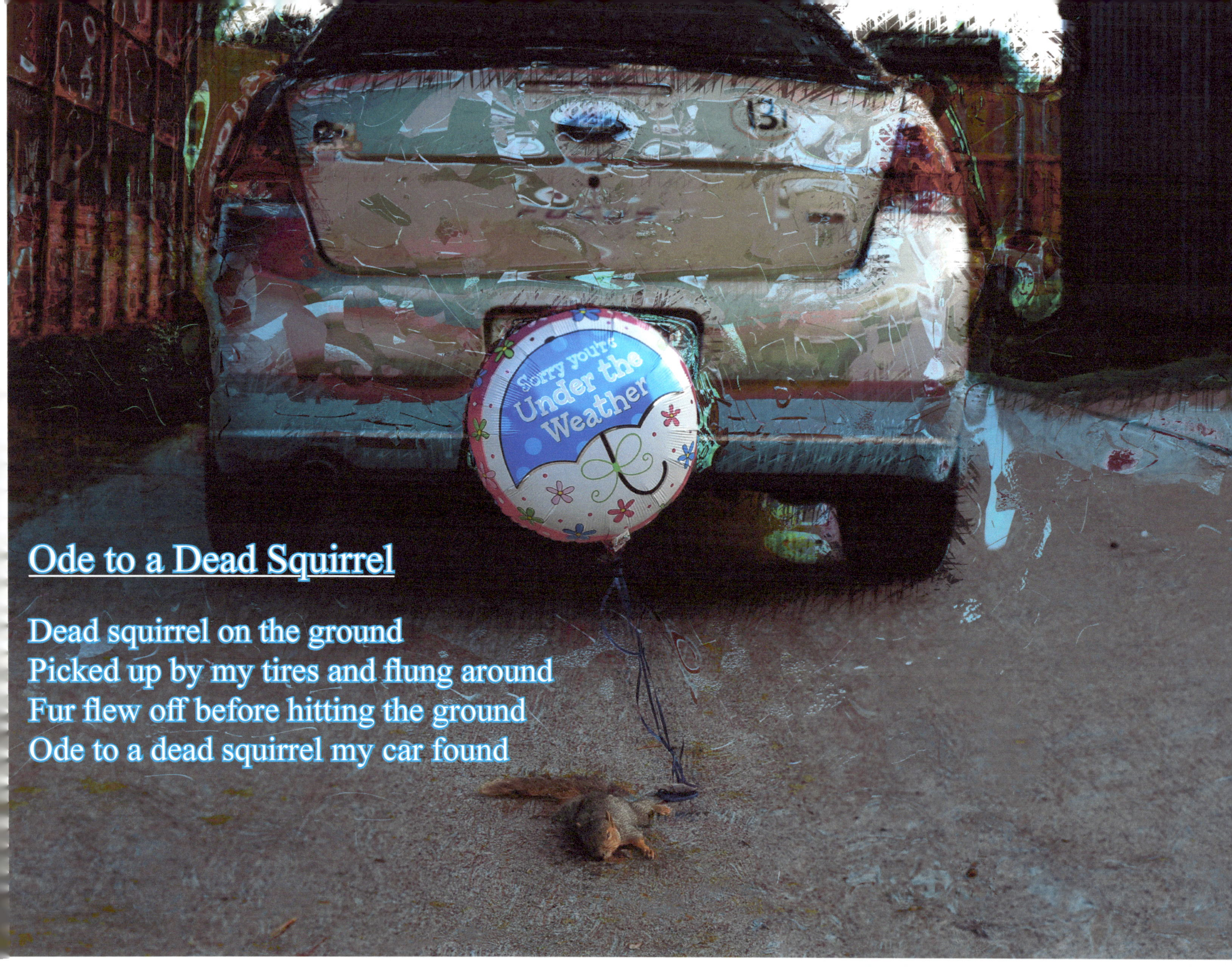

Ode to a Dead Squirrel

Dead squirrel on the ground
Picked up by my tires and flung around
Fur flew off before hitting the ground
Ode to a dead squirrel my car found

Mammals

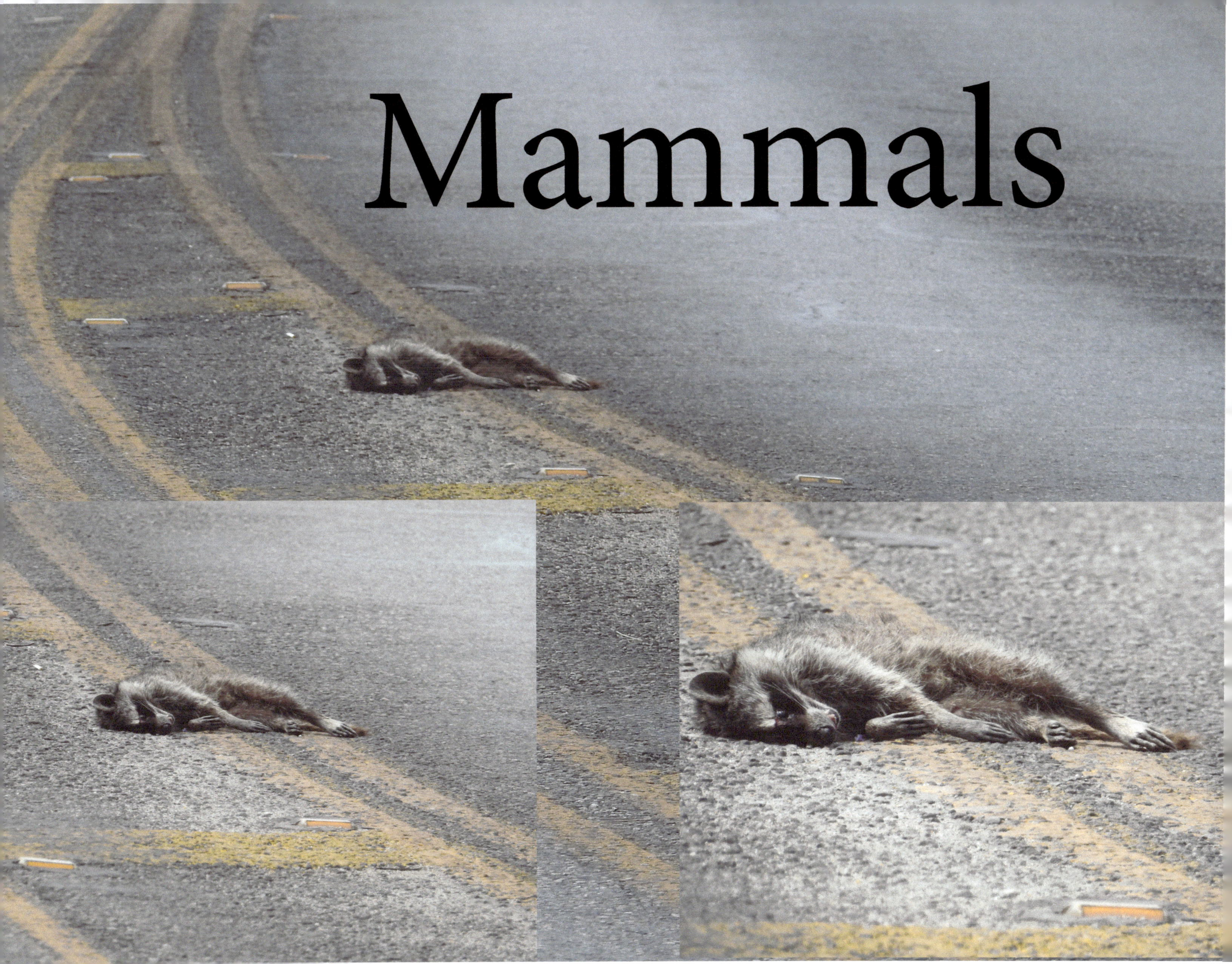

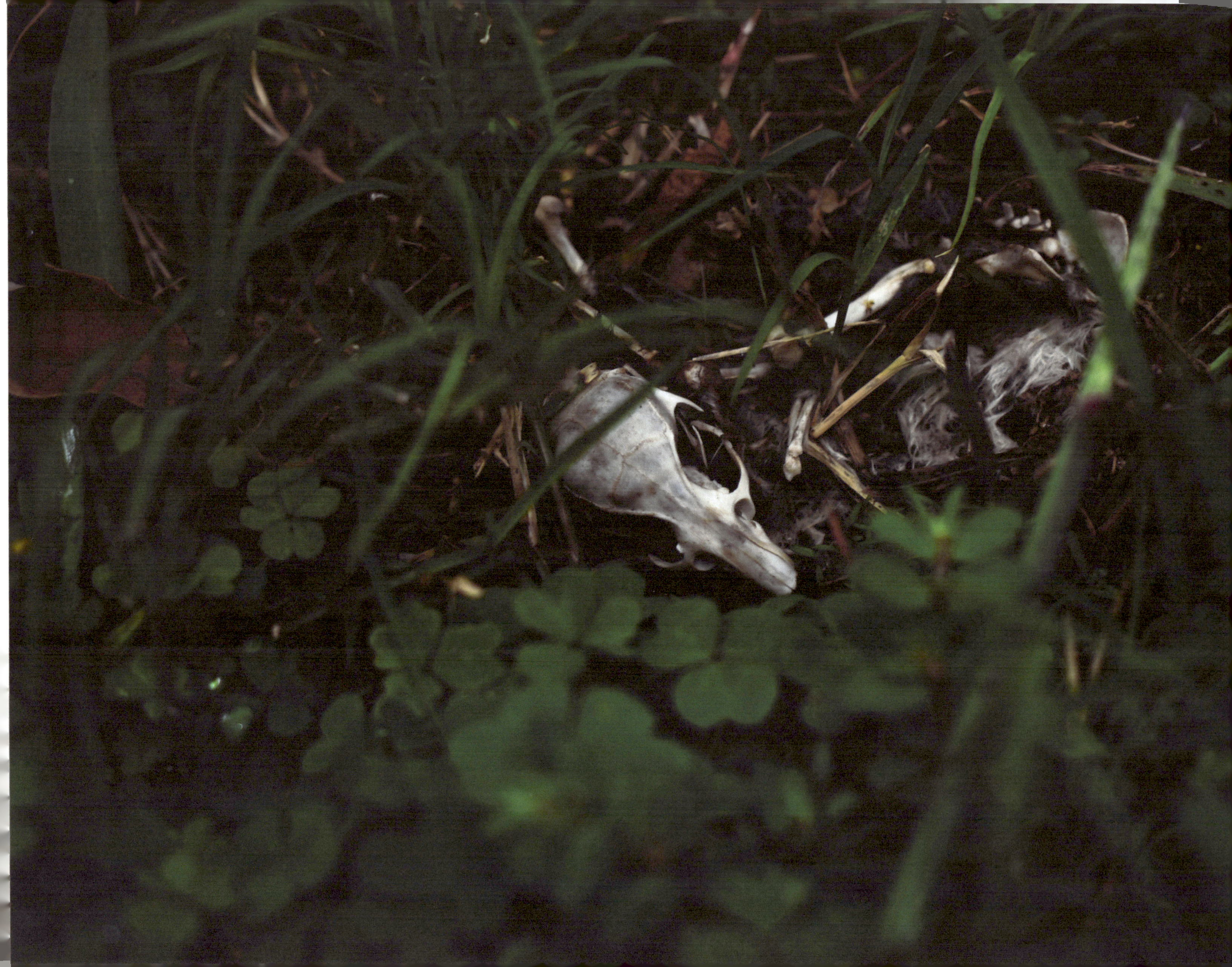

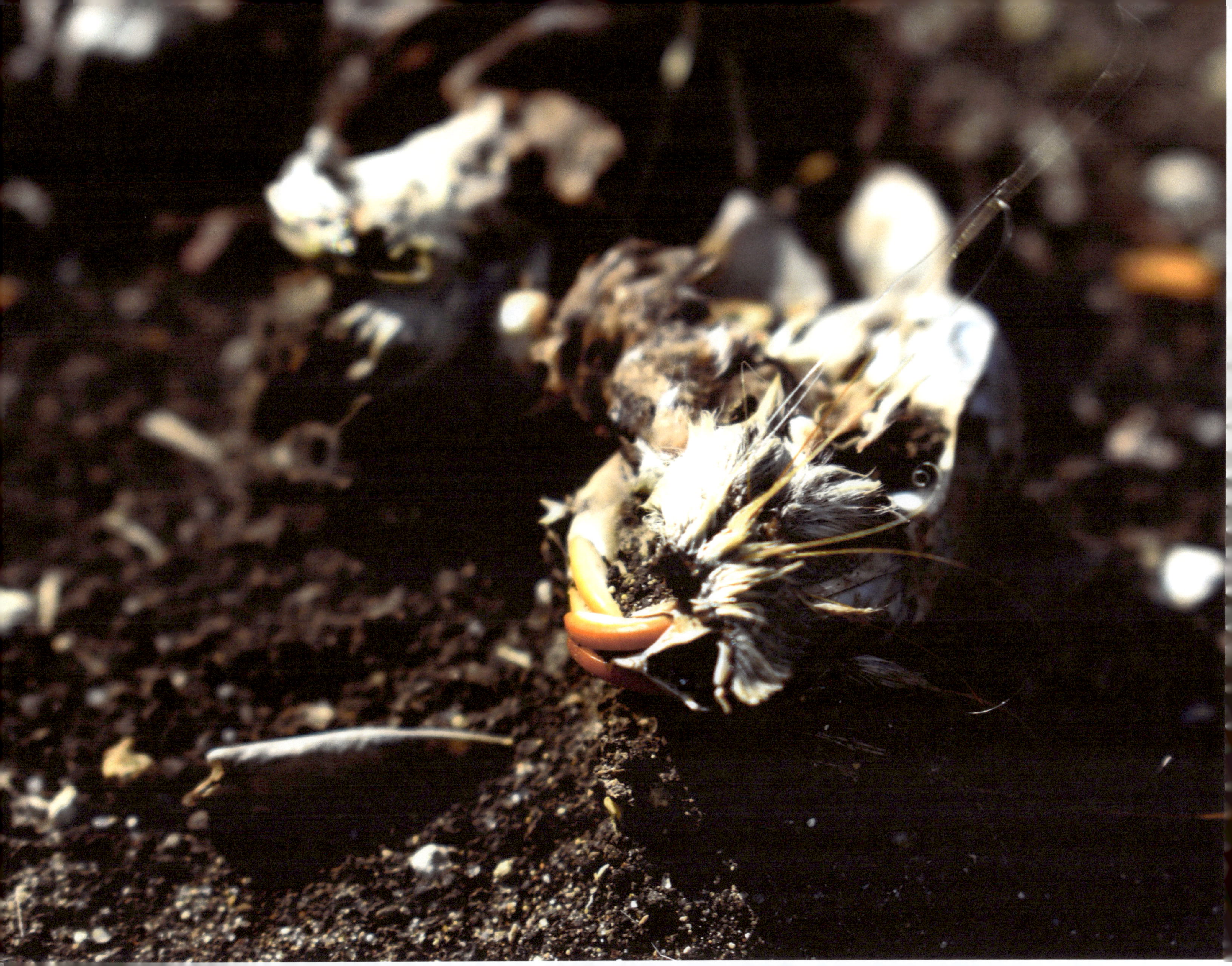

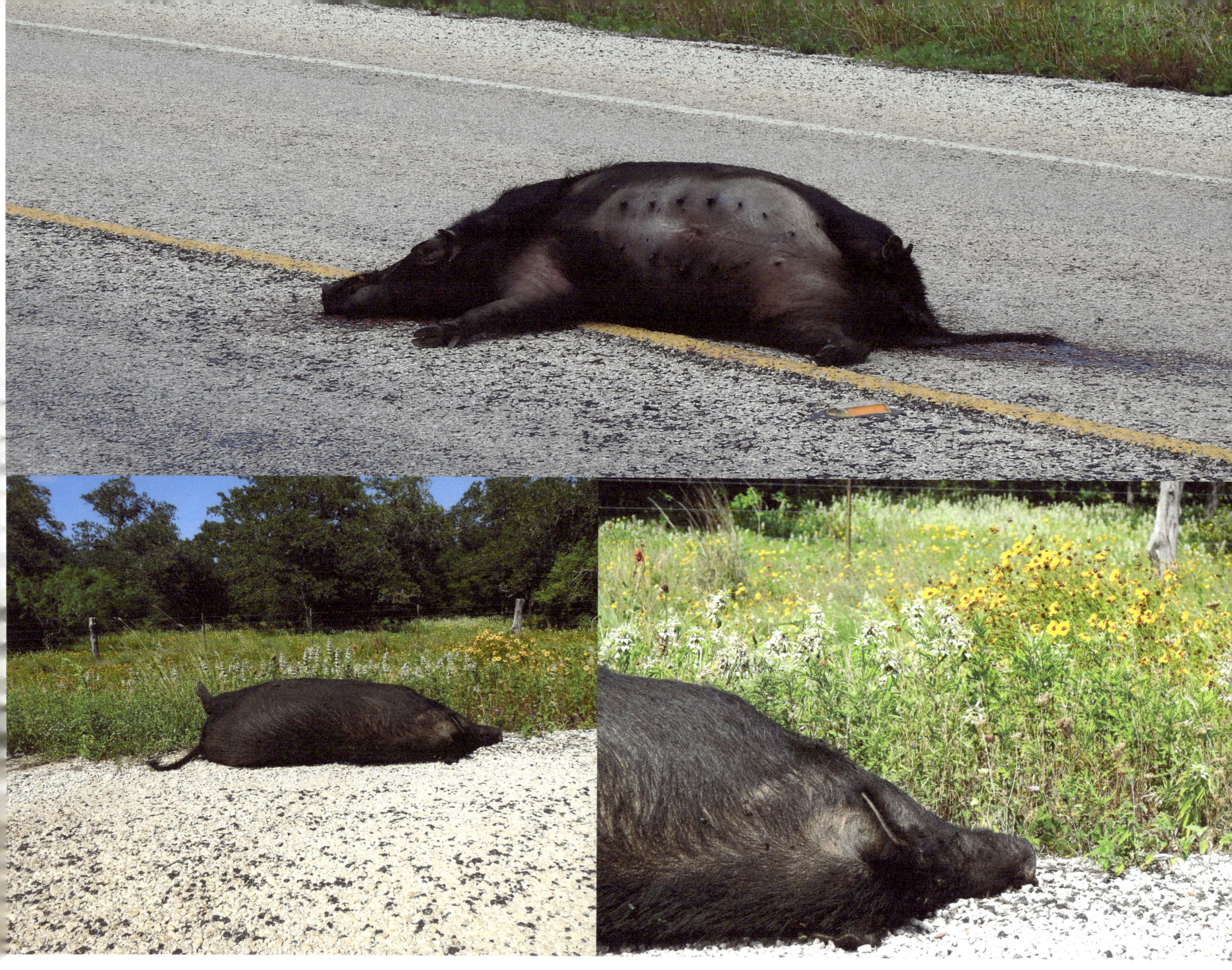

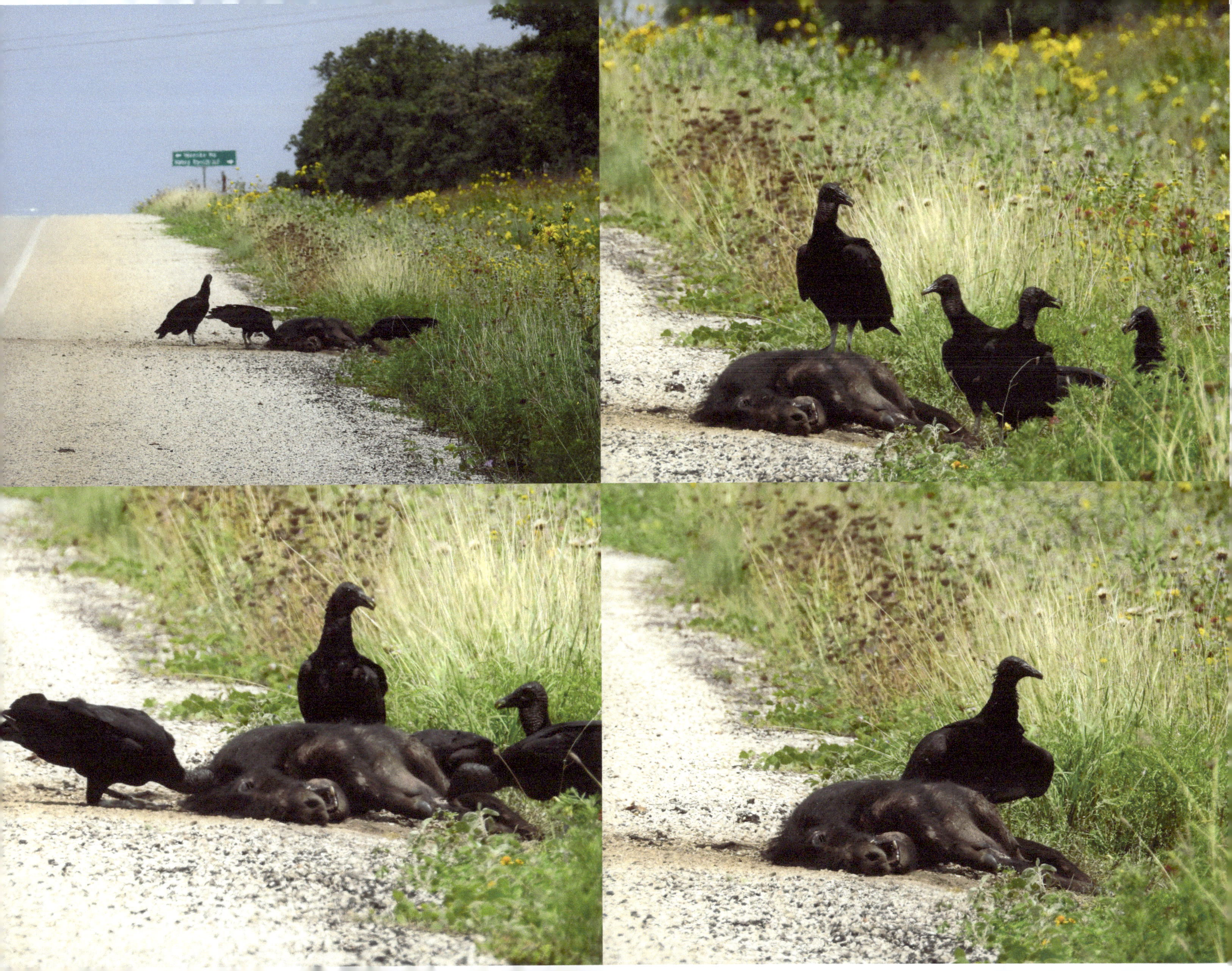

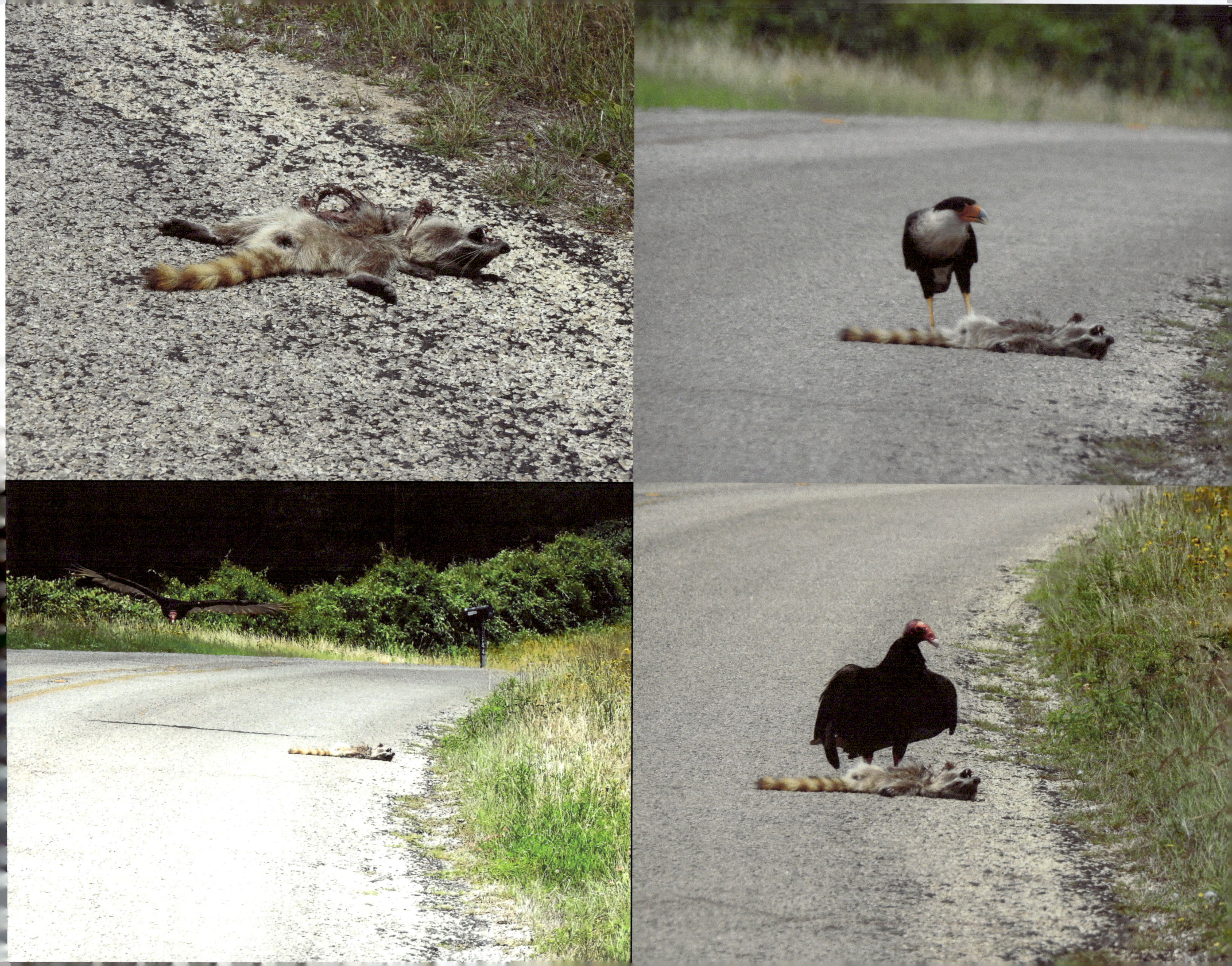

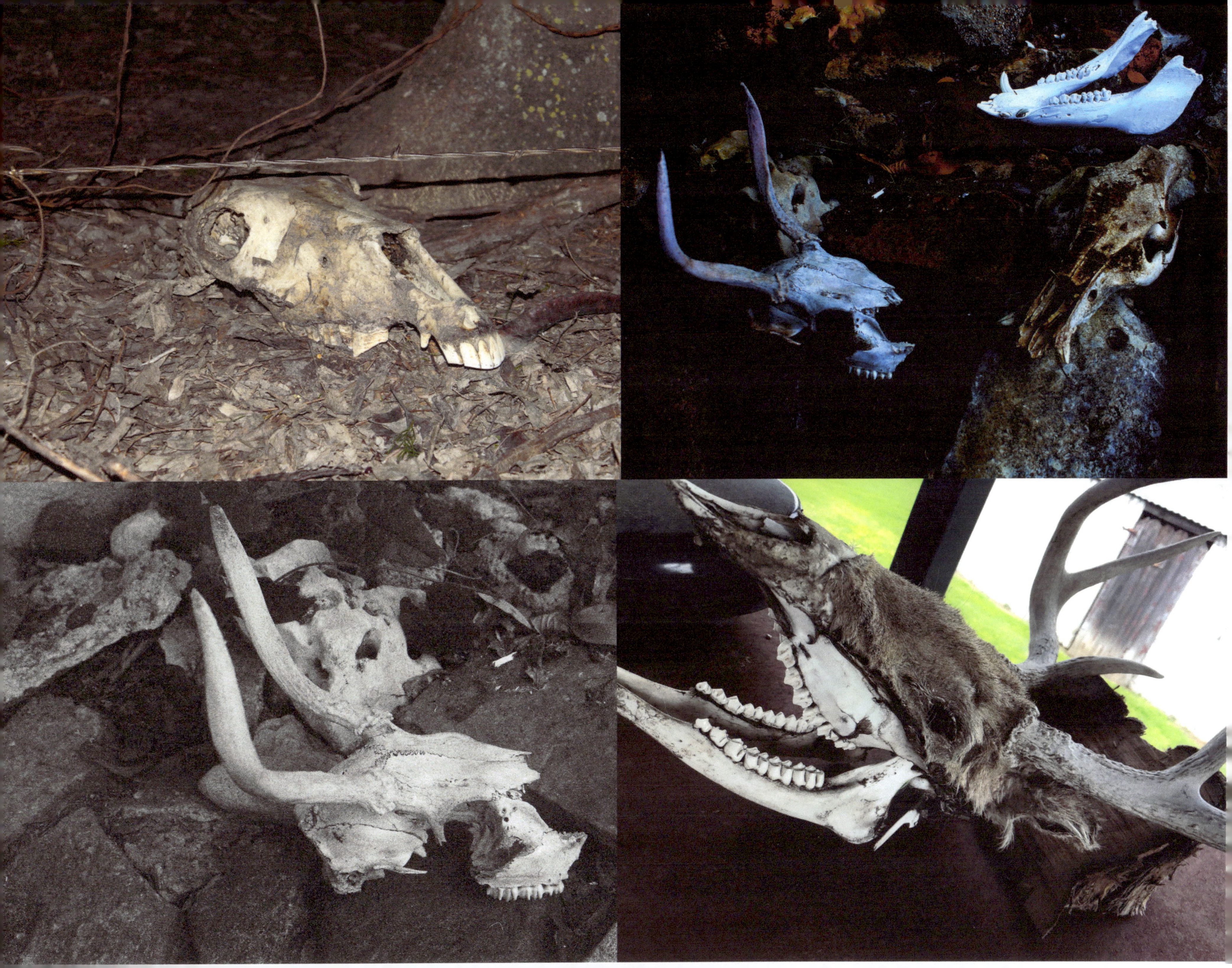

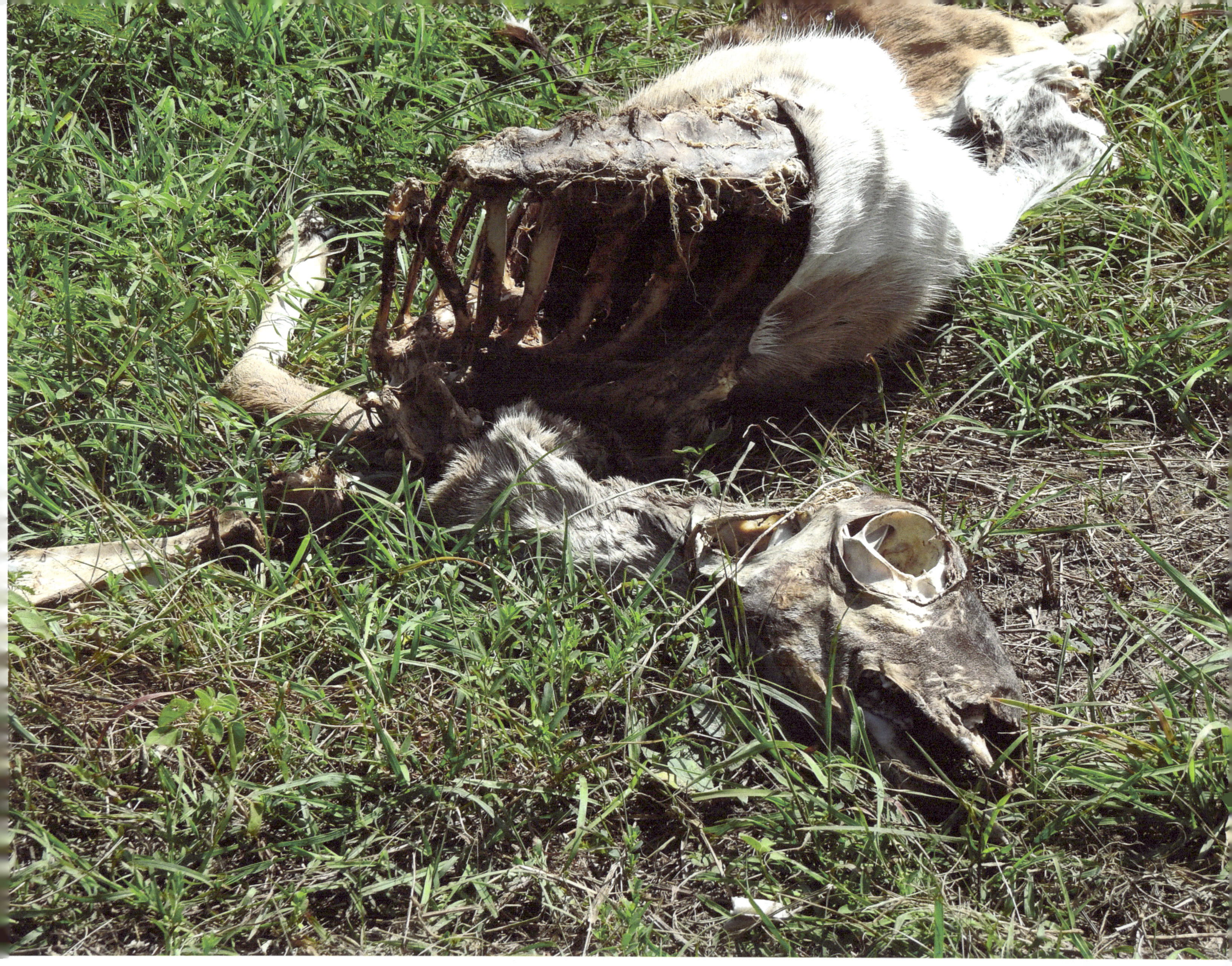

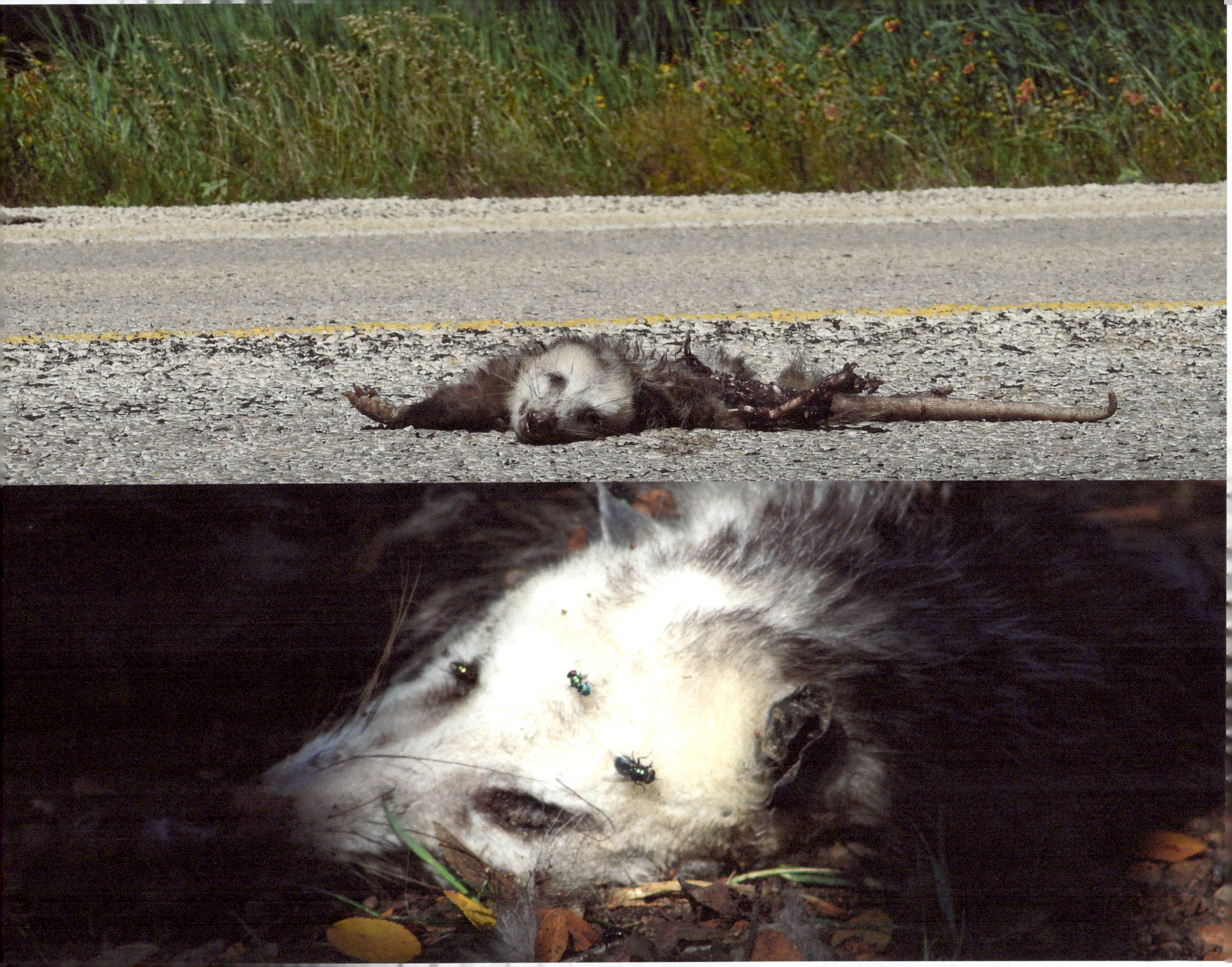

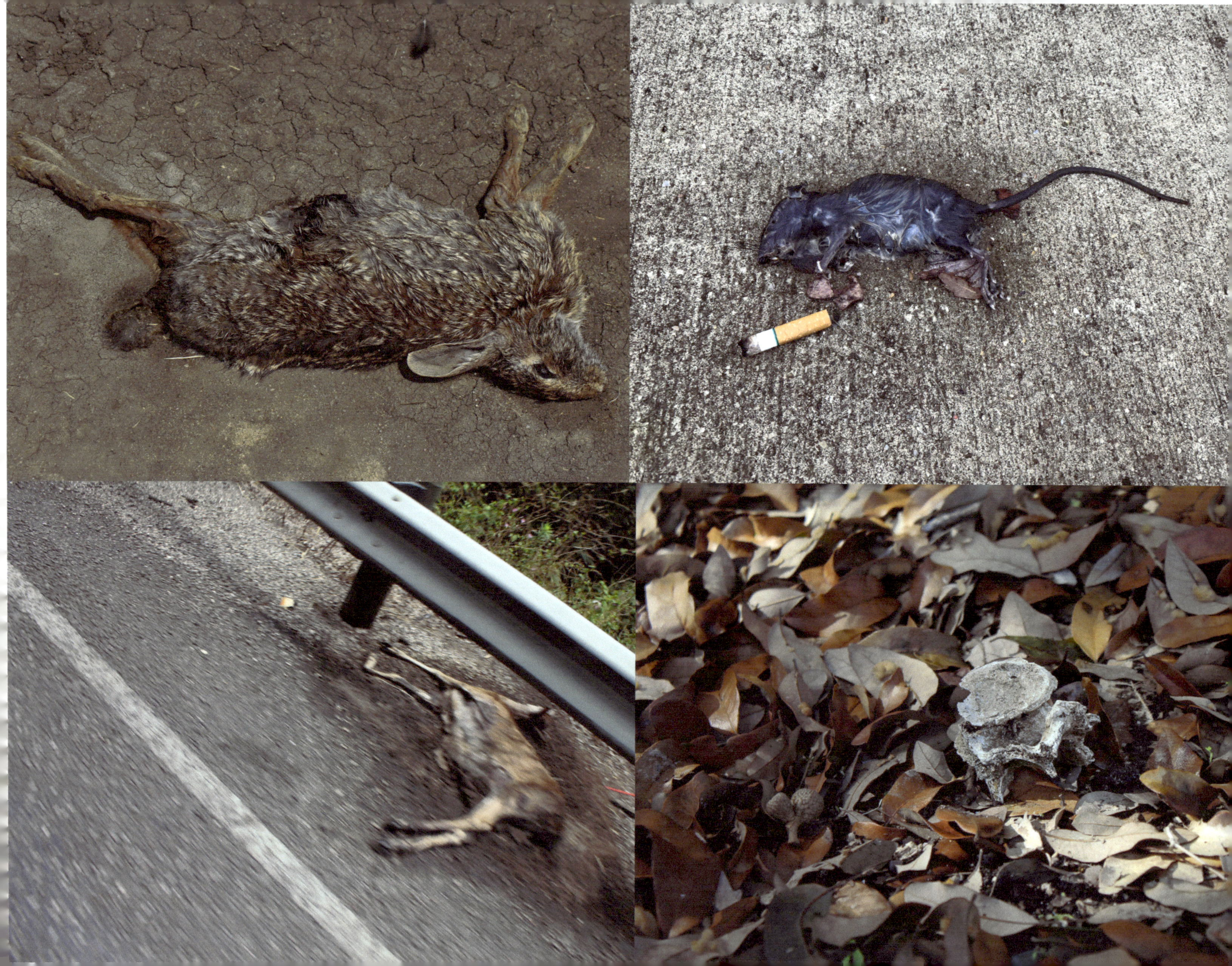

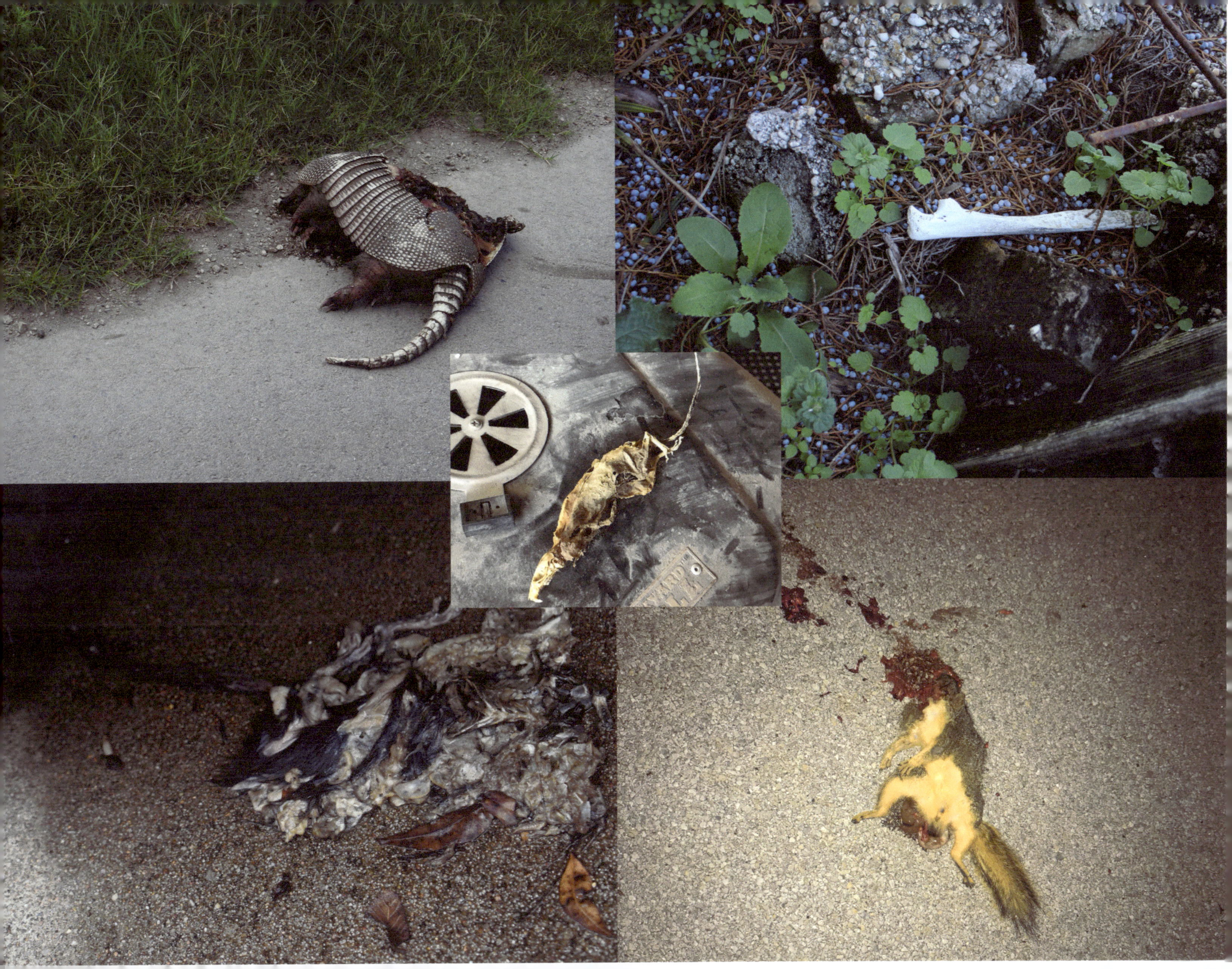

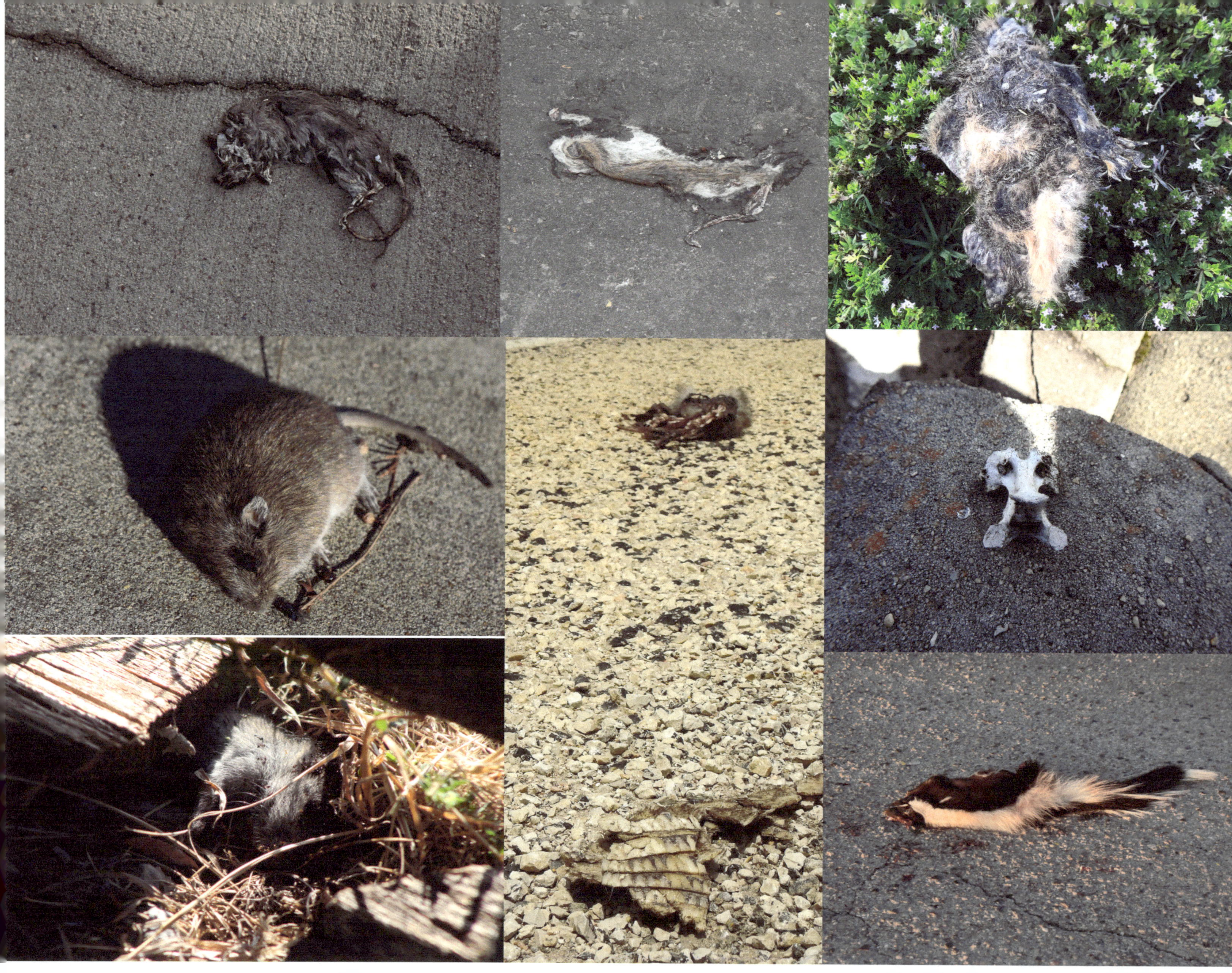

Taxidermy

This is Lord Mousebatton First Earl of Stilton

This is how he came to be...

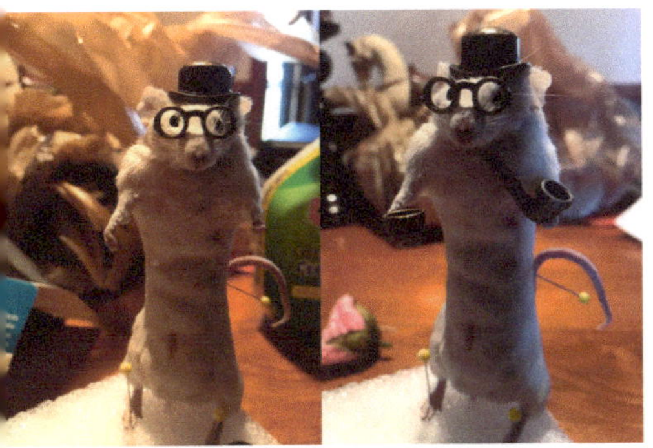

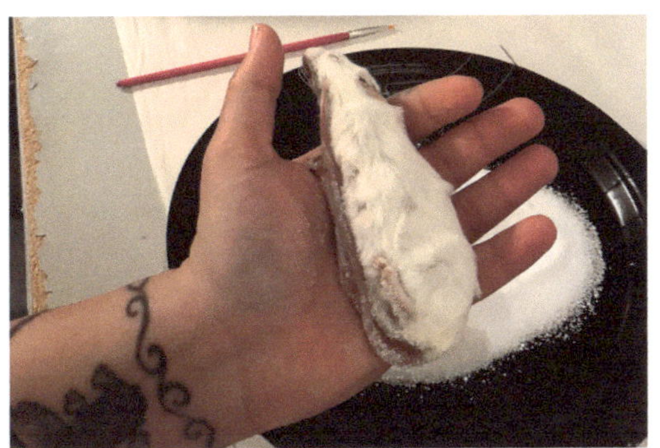

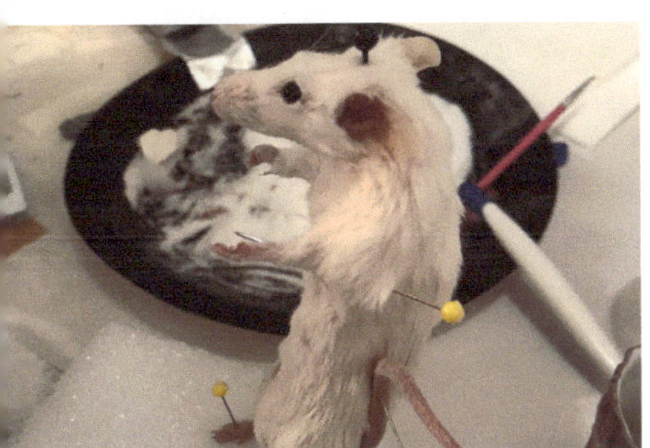

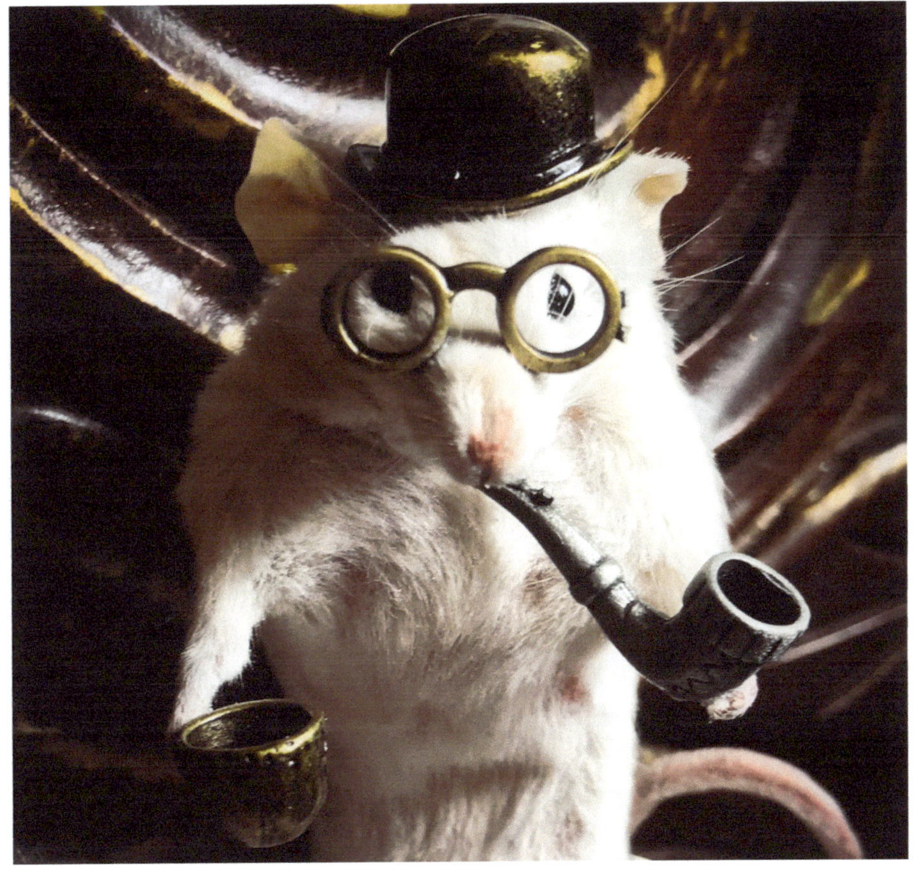

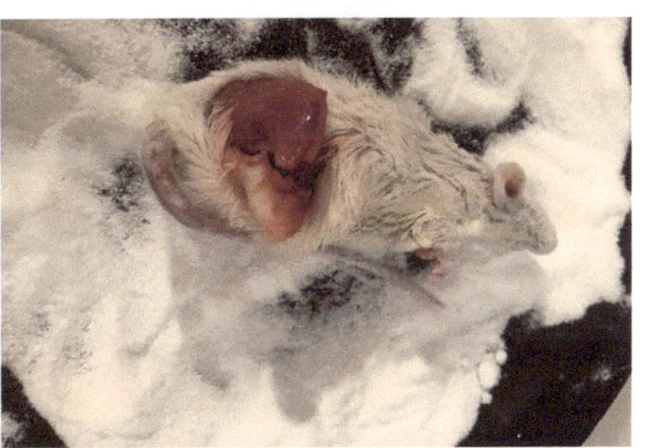

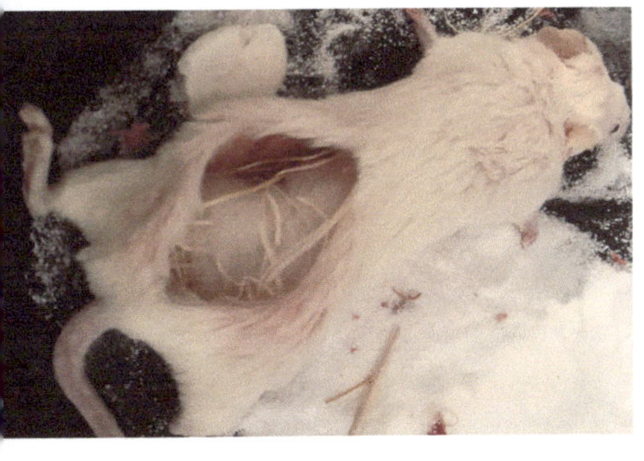

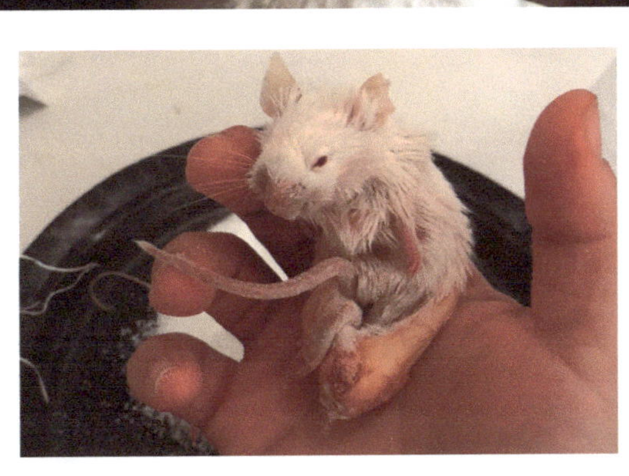

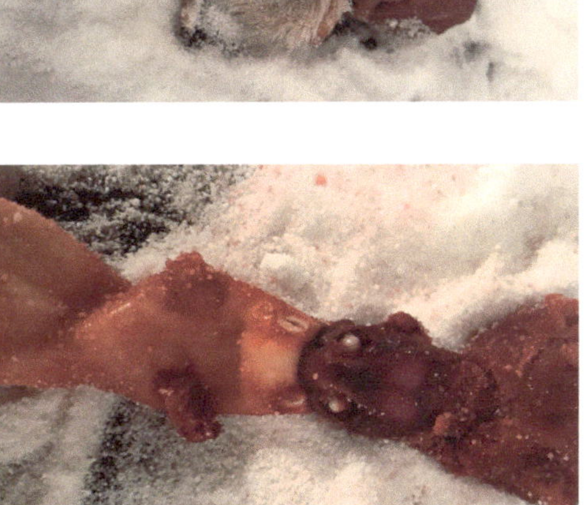

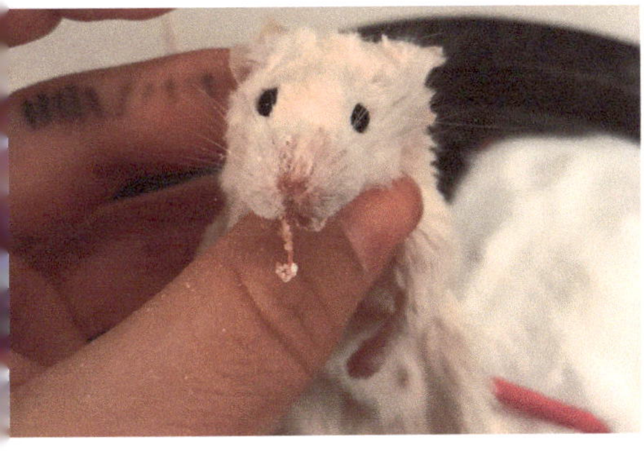

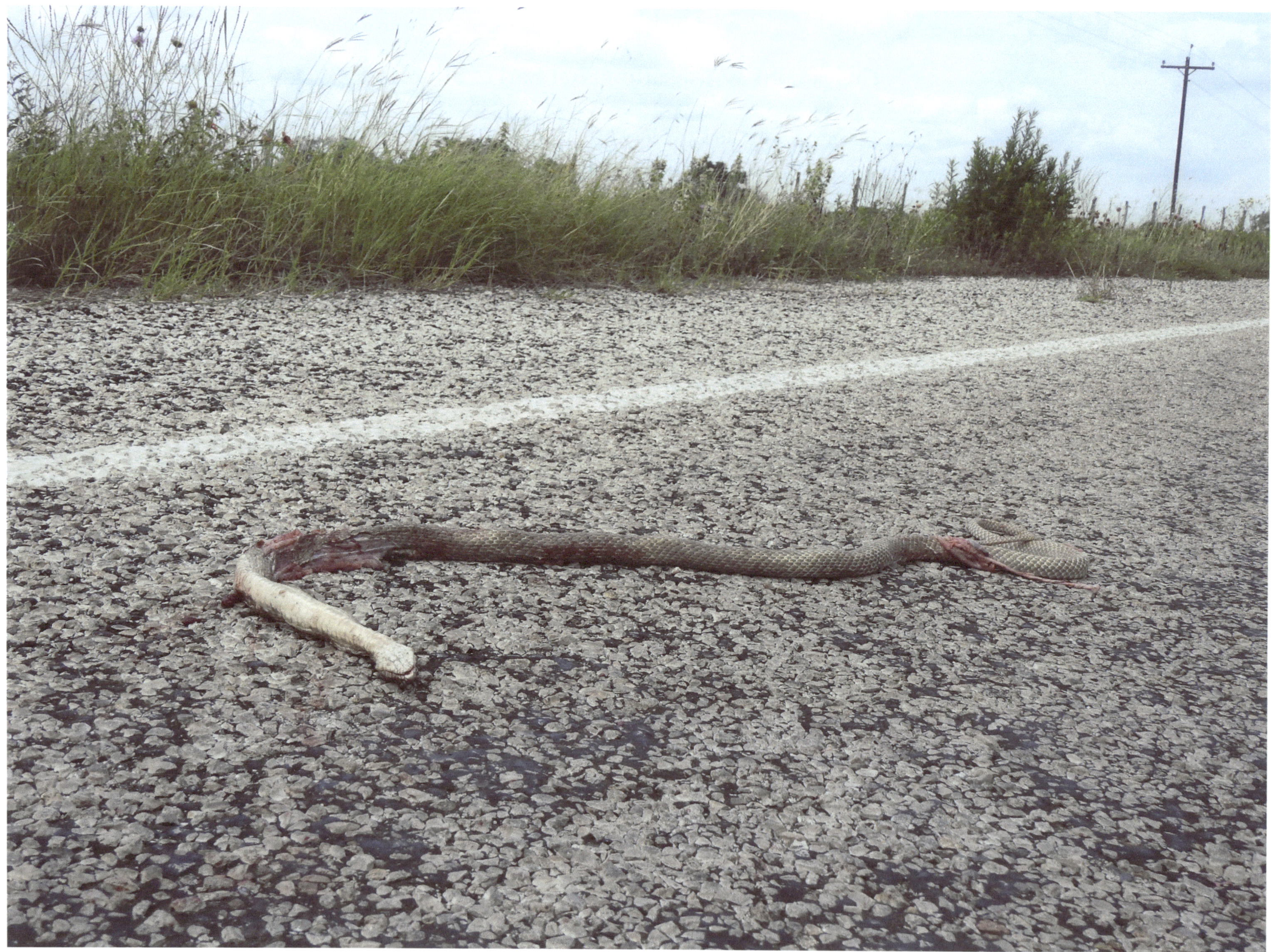

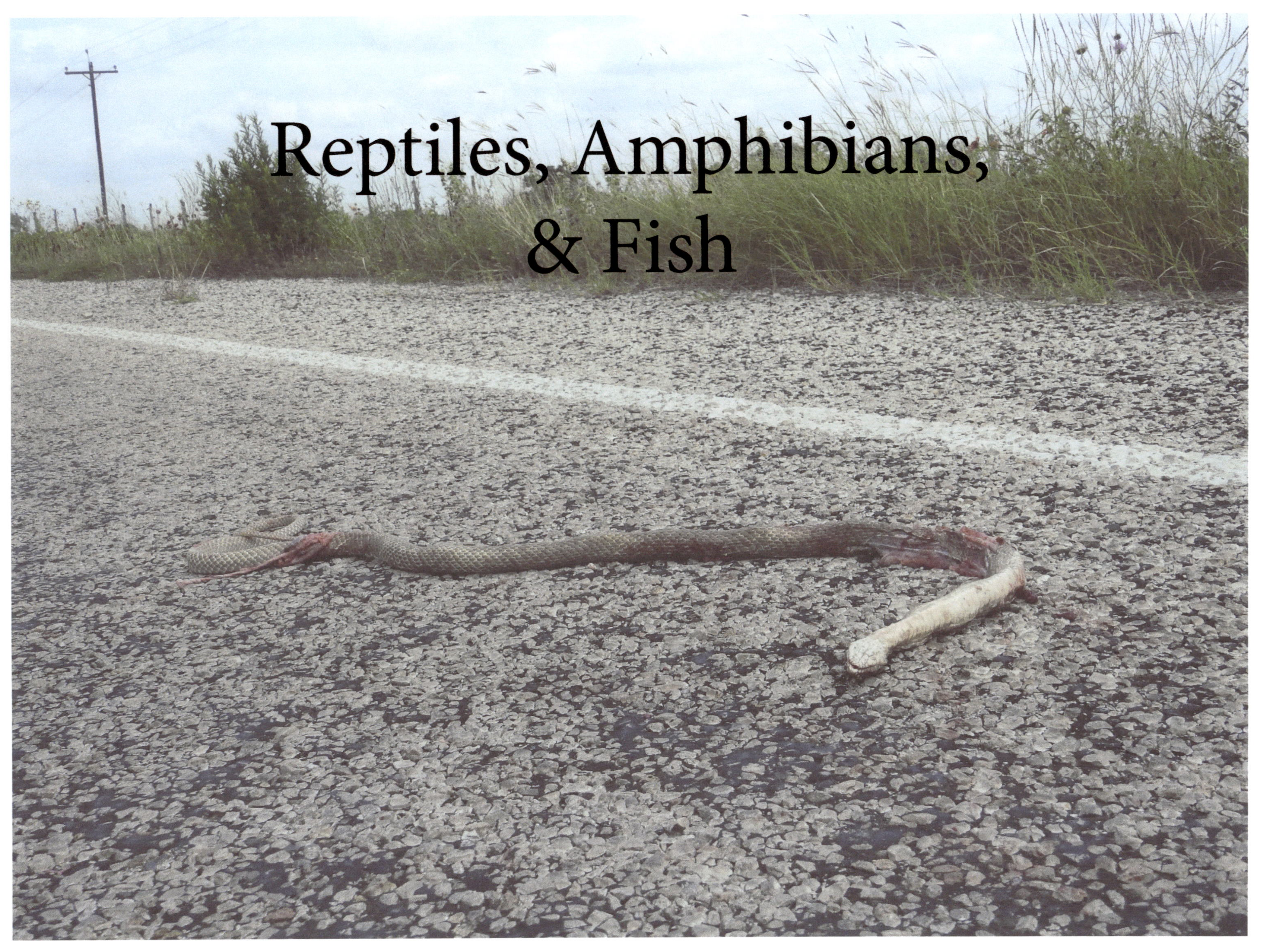
Reptiles, Amphibians,
& Fish

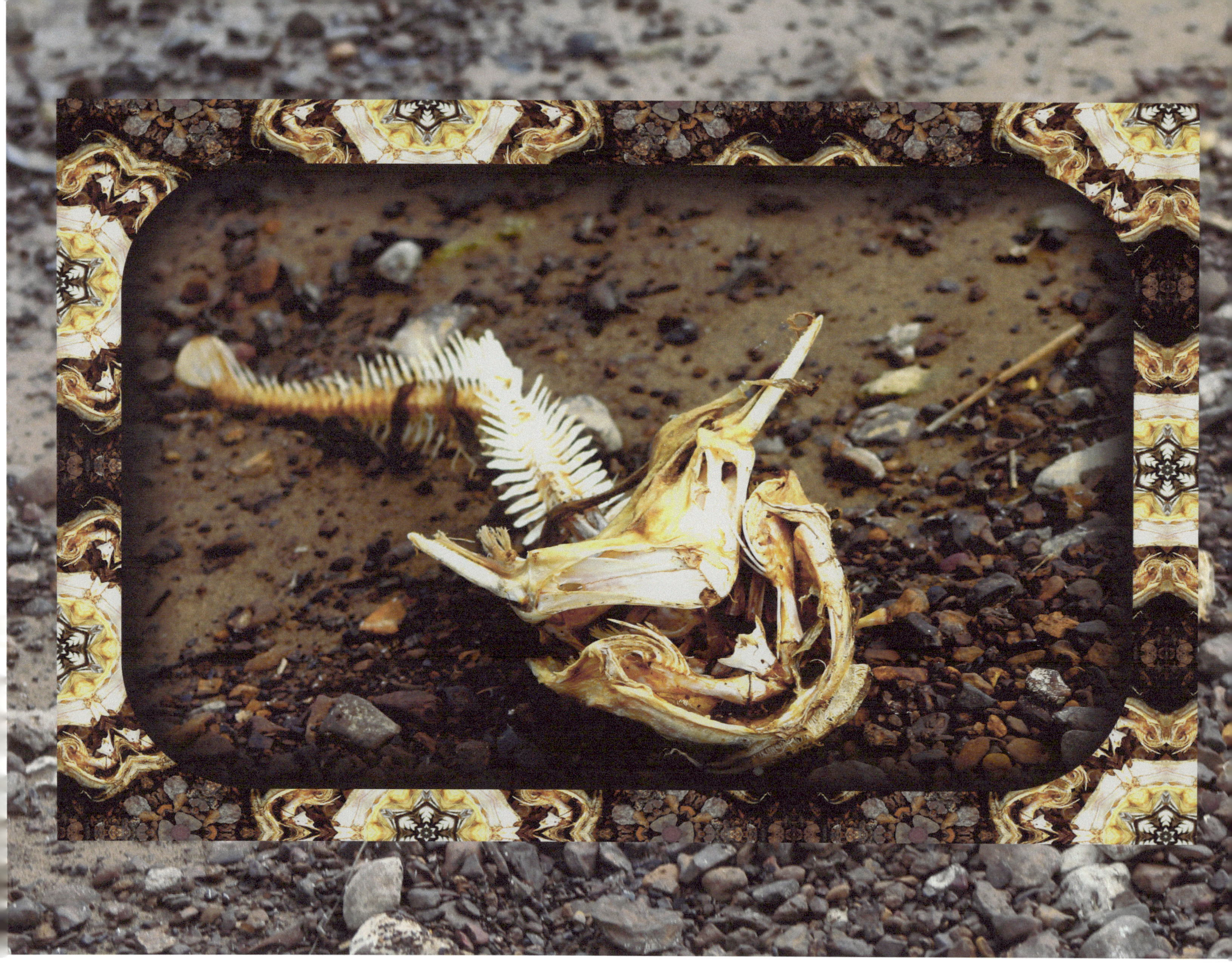

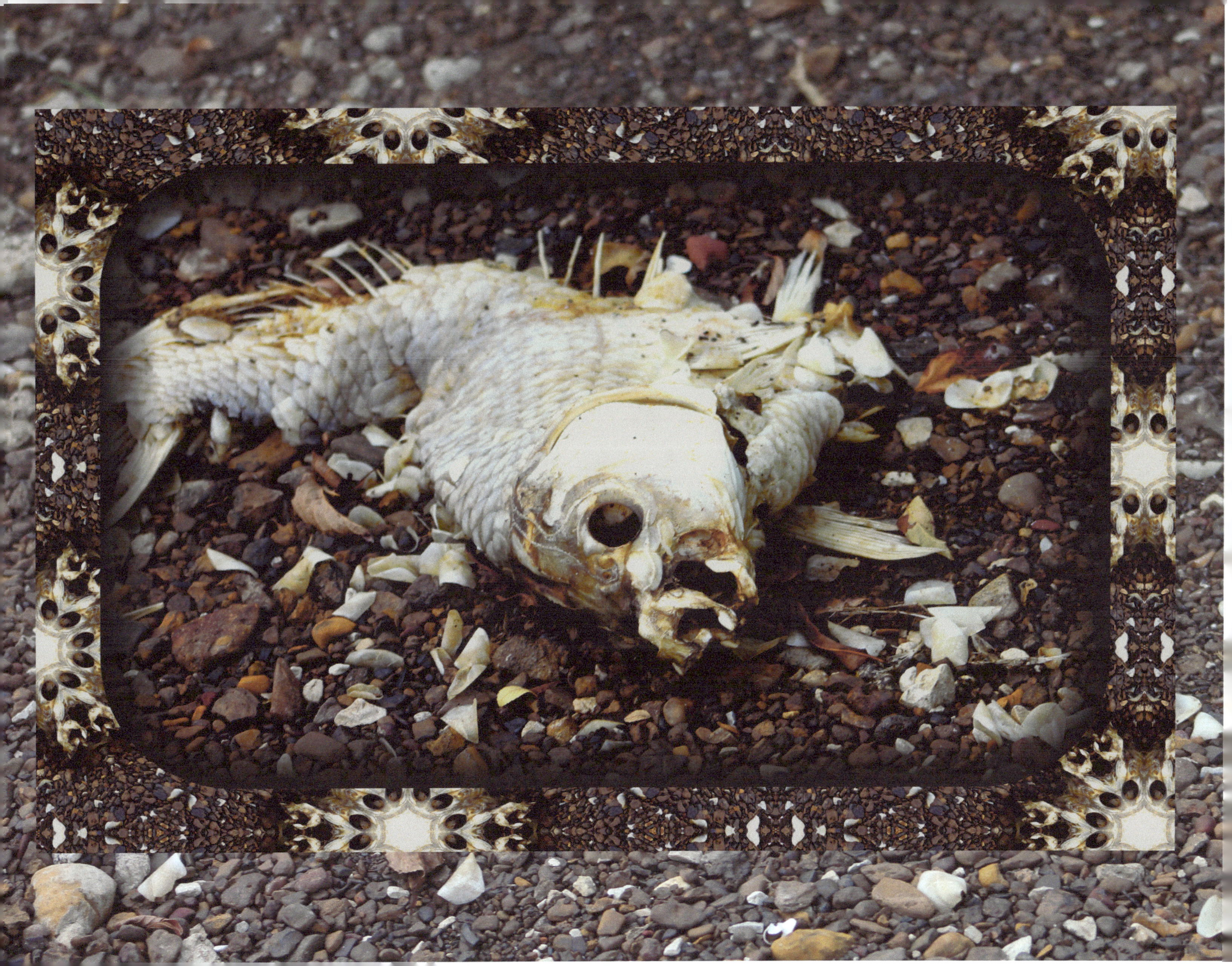

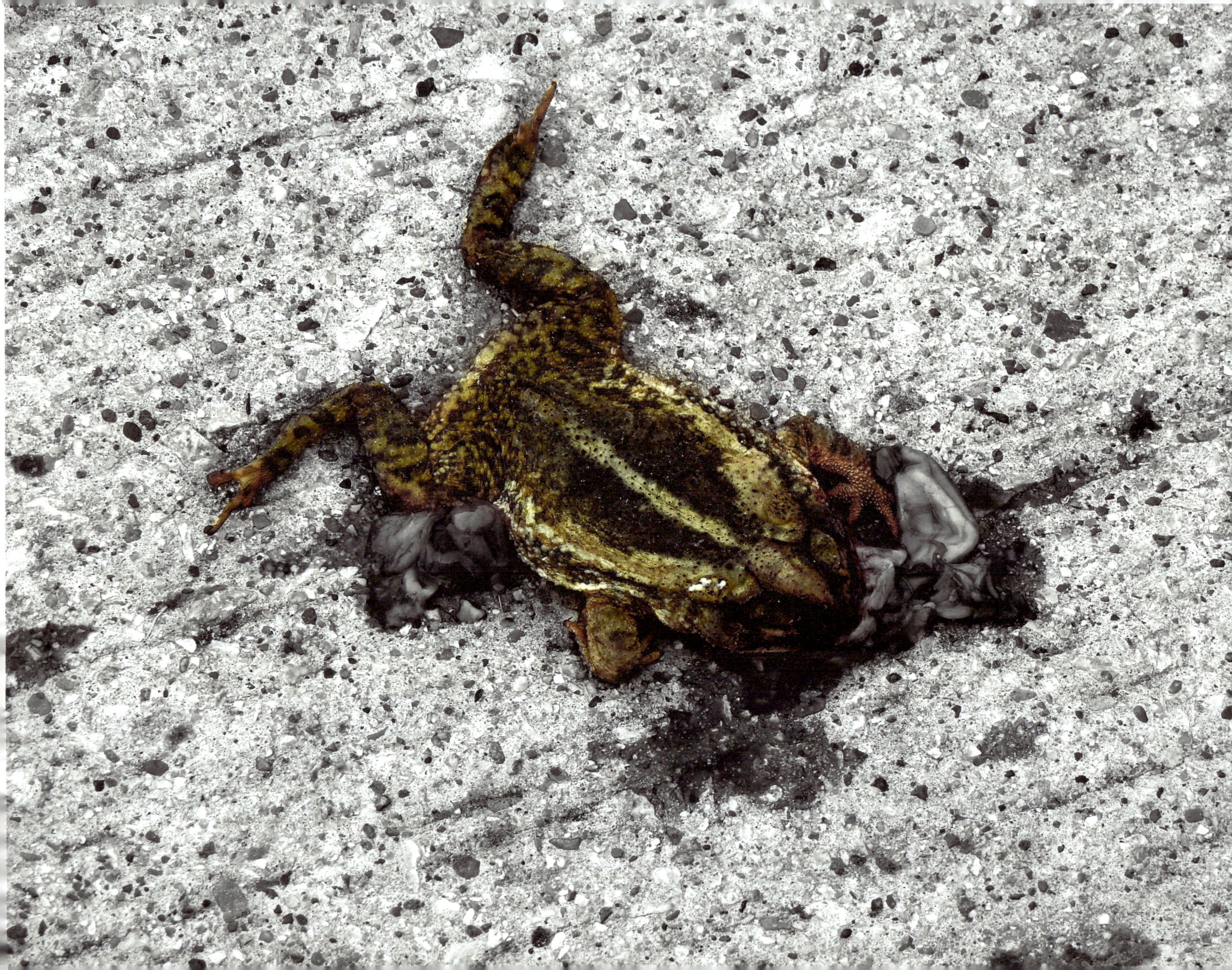

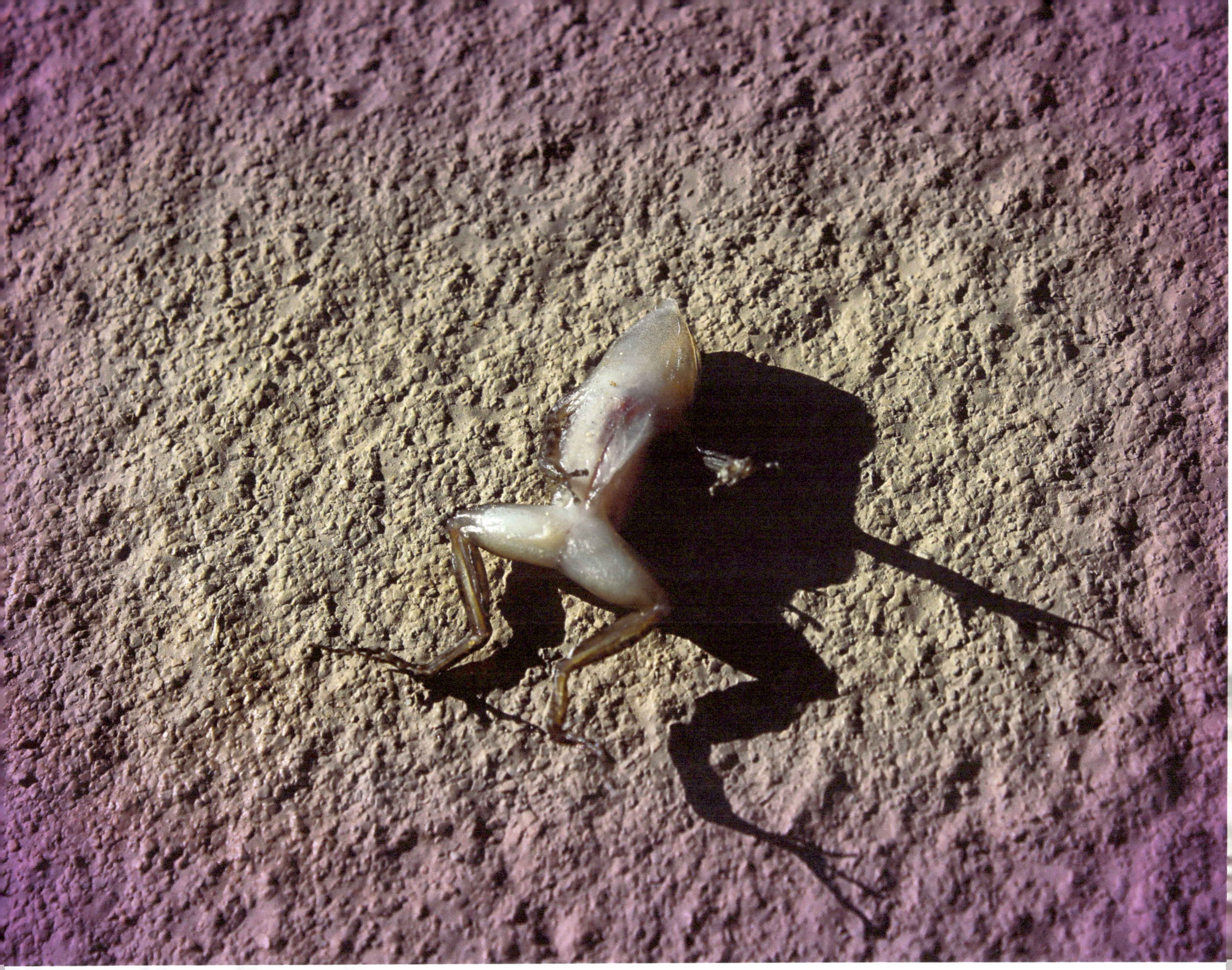

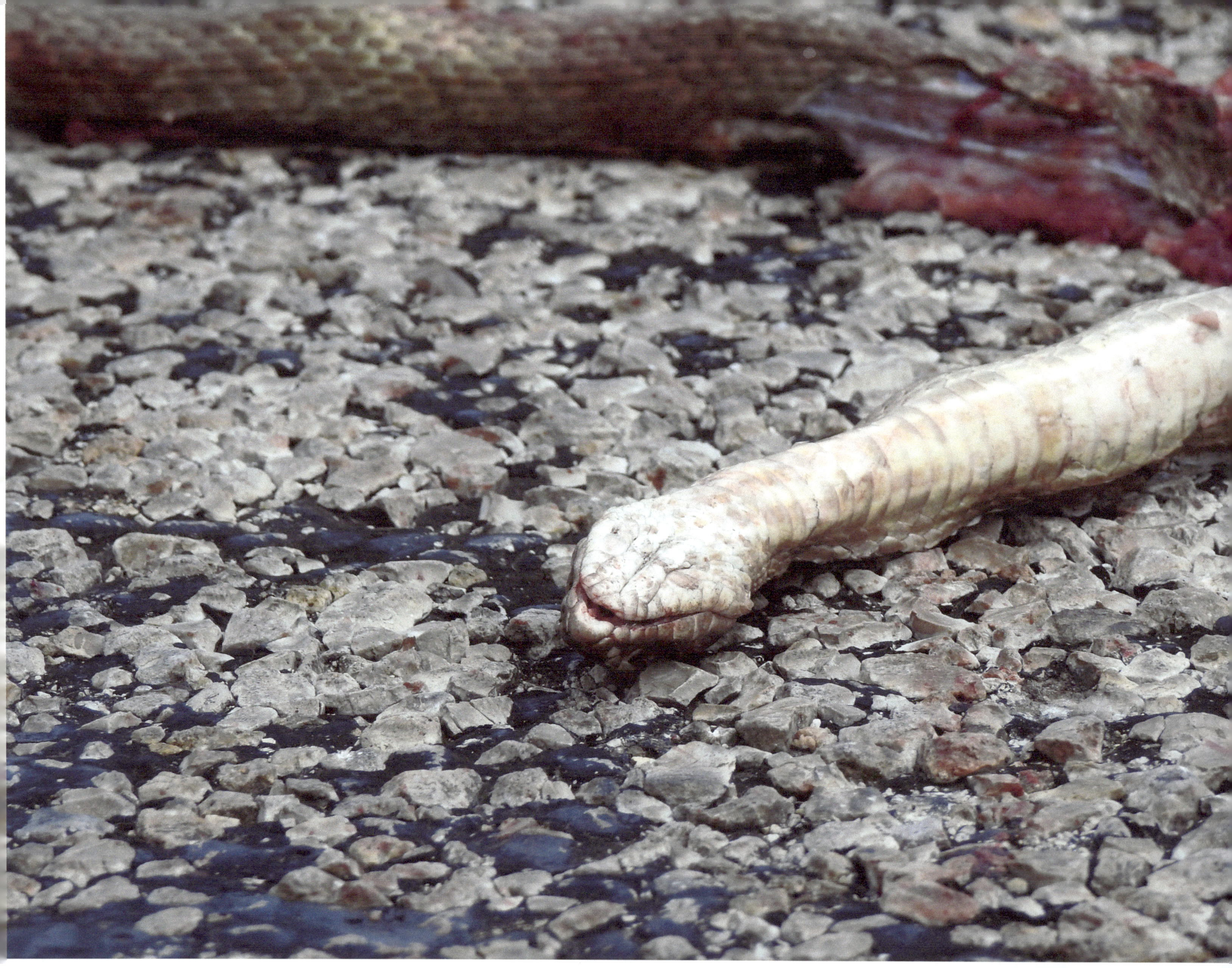

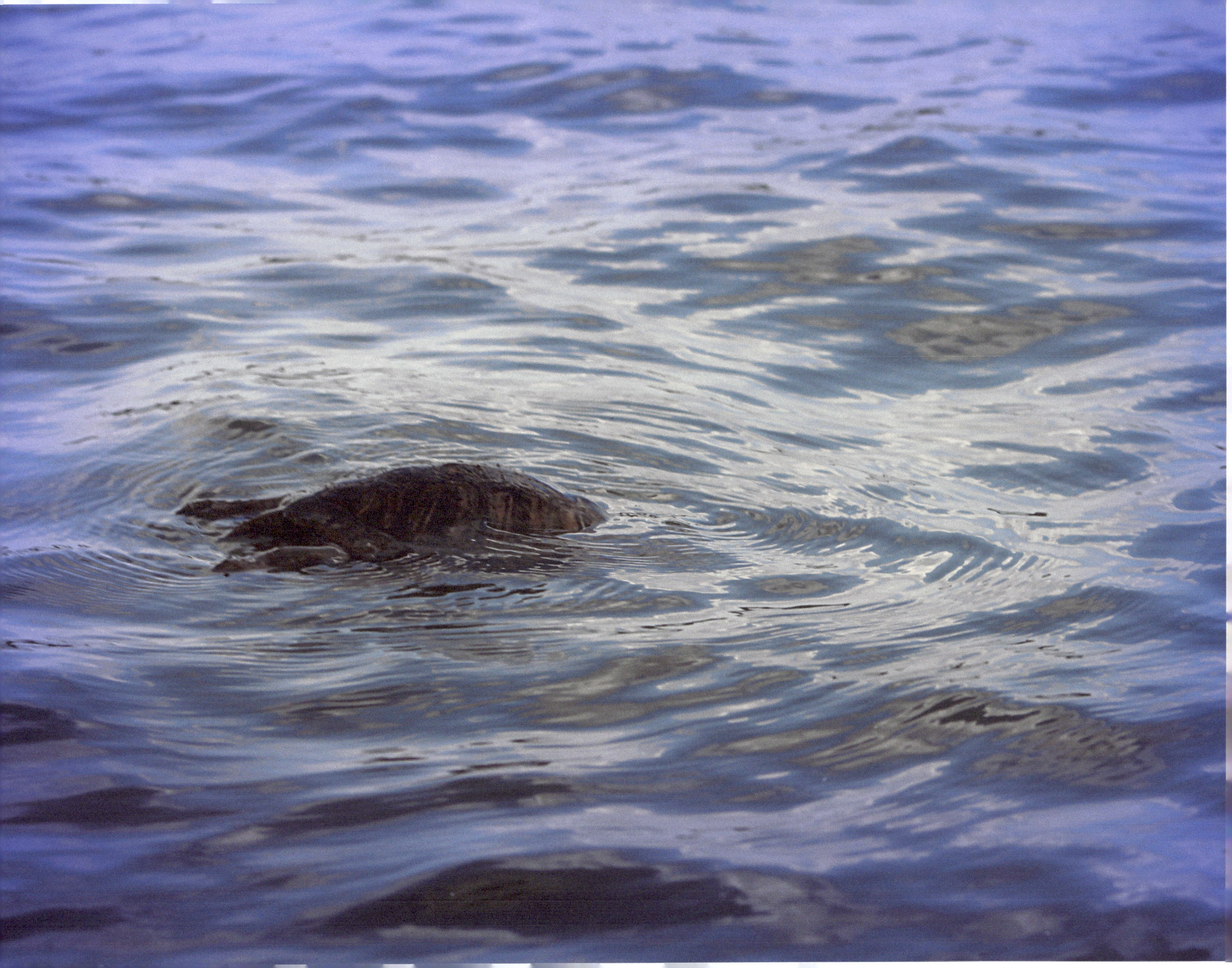